THE MILKY WAY AND OTHER GALAXIES

Edited by
Nicholas Faulkner and Erik Gregersen

Britannica Educational Publishing
IN ASSOCIATION WITH
ROSEN
EDUCATIONAL SERVICES

Published in 2019 by Britannica Educational Publishing (a trademark of Encyclopædia Britannica, Inc.) in association with The Rosen Publishing Group, Inc.
29 East 21st Street, New York, NY 10010

Distributed exclusively by Rosen Publishing.
To see additional Britannica Educational Publishing titles, go to rosenpublishing.com.

Britannica Educational Publishing
J.E. Luebering: Executive Director, Core Editorial
Andrea R. Field: Managing Editor, Compton's by Britannica

Rosen Publishing
Nicholas Faulkner: Editor
Brian Garvey: Series Designer / Book Layout
Cindy Reiman: Photography Manager

Library of Congress Cataloging-in-Publication Data

Names: Faulkner, Nicholas, editor. | Gregersen, Erik, editor.
Title: The Milky Way and other galaxies / edited by Nicholas Faulkner and Erik Gregersen.
Description: New York : Britannica Educational Publishing, in Association with Rosen Educational Services, 2019 | Series: The universe and our place in it | Audience: Grades 7-12. | Includes bibliographical references and index.
Identifiers: LCCN 2018013665| ISBN 9781508106111 (library bound) | ISBN 9781508106104 (pbk.)
Subjects: LCSH: Galaxies—Juvenile literature. | Milky Way—Juvenile literature.
Classification: LCC QB857.3 .M55 2018 | DDC 523.1/12—dc23
LC record available at https://lccn.loc.gov/2018013665

Manufactured in the United States of America

Photo credits: Cover (top), p. 1 Carlos Fernandez/Moment/Getty Images; cover (bottom) tose/Shutterstock.com; p. 8 Robert Williams and the Hubble Deep Field Team (STScI) and NASA; p. 10 Vaclav Janousek/Fotolia; pp. 12, 96 The Hubble Heritage Team (AURA/ STScI/ NASA); p. 15 European Space Agency and NASA; p. 19 Courtesy of Palomar Observatory/California Institute of Technology; p. 21 NASA, C.R. O'Dell and S.K. Wong (Rice University); p. 22 J.P. Harrington and K.J. Borkowski (University of Maryland), and NASA; pp. 25, 84 NASA, ESA, and The Hubble Heritage Team (STScI/AURA); p. 29 R. Gilmozzi, Space Telescope Science Institute/European Space Agency; Shawn Ewald, JPL; and NASA; p. 32 Viktar Malyshchyts/Shutterstock.com; pp. 36, 102 NASA; p. 38 © AAS. Reproduced with permission; pp. 44-45 NOAO/AURA/NSF; p. 48 NASA, ESA, S. Beckwith (STScI), and The Hubble Heritage Team (STScI/AURA); p. 62 Local Group Galaxies Survey Team/NOAO/AURA/NSF; p. 71 GALEX Team, Caltech, NASA; p. 73 Encyclopædia Britannica, Inc.; p. 76 CFHT/NOAO/AURA/NSF/NASA/ESA/STScI; p. 78 NOAO/Science Source; p. 79 © WIYN Consortium, Inc. 3.5-m Telescope/C. Howk, JHU/ B. Savage, U. Wisconsin/N. Sharp, WIYN/NOAO/AURA/NSF; p. 86 Visuals Unlimited, Inc./Robert Gendler/Visuals Unlimited/Getty Images; p. 97 Reinhold Wittich/Stocktrek Images/Getty Images; p. 98 Prof. Vincent Icke/Science Source; p. 100 B. Whitmore (STScI)—NASA/ESA; p. 108 The Hubble Heritage Team; interior pages background (blue triangles) DiamondGraphics/Shutterstock.com.

CONTENTS

CHAPTER 2

CHAPTER 3

INTRODUCTION

Virtually all galaxies appear to have been formed soon after the universe began, approximately 13 billion years ago. Measurements tend to suggest that most, if not all, galaxies have very nearly the same age and that they consist of stars and interstellar matter—clouds of gas and particles of dust—that move together through space. Even small galaxies contain millions of stars, while the largest may have trillions of stars. And the universe is made up of trillions of galaxies, which are found all over the sky, even in the depths of the farthest reaches penetrated by powerful modern telescopes. The Sun and the solar system, including Earth, are part of the Milky Way Galaxy.

The Milky Way Galaxy is a large spiral system consisting of several hundred billion stars. It takes its name from the Milky Way, the irregular luminous band of stars and gas clouds that stretches across the sky as seen from Earth. Every star that can be seen from Earth without a telescope belongs to the Milky Way Galaxy.

The Milky Way Galaxy is an example of a spiral galaxy, which are shaped like pinwheels and have immense spiral arms. The Sun (as well as Earth) is located on the inner edge of a spiral arm,

This image, the result of 10 days' observation by the Hubble Space Telescope, shows 1,500 galaxies in different stages of their evolution.

some 27,000 light-years from the nucleus, or centre, of the Galaxy. The Galaxy's disk and spiral arms have a diameter of roughly 100,000 light-years. The Sun and all the other stars of the Galaxy take about 200 million years to orbit about the nucleus.

Galaxies vary greatly in size and grow by colliding and merging with other galaxies. Some extreme dwarf galaxies found near the Milky Way Galaxy are only 100 light-years across, while large spiral galaxies typically have diameters of 100,000 to 500,000 light-years. On the other hand, giant radio galaxies, which are very strong sources of radio waves, extend more than 3,000,000 light-years.

Most galaxies move through the universe in clusters, sometimes in small groups and sometimes in enormous complexes. Isolated galaxies are quite rare. The Milky Way Galaxy, for example, belongs to the Local Group, which also includes the Magellanic Clouds, the Andromeda Galaxy, and about 50 other galaxies.

Evidence suggests that at the centre of many galaxies lies a supermassive black hole, a region of such intense gravity that nothing, not even light, can escape. Additionally, when two galaxies merge, their nuclei—and black holes—collide, generating an immense amount of energy. At the centre of the Galaxy is a massive black hole, named Sagittarius A*, and it has a mass about 4.3 million times larger than the Sun's.

In the late 20th century a surprising finding was made—most of the mass in galaxies is not in the form of stars or other visible matter. Most galaxies have much more mass than can be accounted for by their stars. This means that they must contain some "dark matter," from which no light is seen. The nature of this dark matter is not yet known.

This text studies the nature of the various types of galaxies, including our own. Scientists have only begun to understand the complexities of these immense celestial networks.

CHAPTER 1

THE MILKY WAY

The Milky Way Galaxy is the galaxy that we call home. Although Earth lies well within the Milky Way, astronomers do not have as complete an understanding of its nature as they do of some external star systems. A thick layer of interstellar dust obscures much of

Artist's rendition of the Milky Way Galaxy.

the Galaxy from scrutiny by optical telescopes, and astronomers can determine its large-scale structure only with the aid of radio and infrared telescopes, which can detect the forms of radiation that penetrate the obscuring matter.

Although most stars in the Milky Way Galaxy exist either as single stars like the Sun or as double stars, there are many conspicuous groups and clusters of stars that contain tens to thousands of members. These objects can be subdivided into three types: globular clusters, open clusters, and stellar associations. They differ primarily in age and in the number of member stars.

GLOBULAR CLUSTERS

The largest and most massive star clusters are the globular clusters, so called because of their roughly spherical appearance. The Galaxy contains more than 150 globular clusters (the exact number is uncertain because of obscuration by dust in the Milky Way band, which probably prevents some globular clusters from being seen). They are arranged in a nearly spherical halo around the Milky Way, with relatively few toward the galactic plane but a heavy concentration toward the centre. The radial distribution, when plotted as a function of distance from the galactic centre, fits a mathematical expression of a form identical to the one describing the star distribution in elliptical galaxies.

Globular cluster M80 (also known as NGC 6093) in an optical image taken by the Hubble Space Telescope. M80 is located 28,000 light-years from Earth.

Globular clusters are extremely luminous objects. Their mean luminosity is the equivalent of approximately 25,000 Suns. The most luminous are 50 times brighter. The masses of globular clusters, measured by determining the dispersion in the velocities of individual stars, range from a few thousand to more than 1,000,000 solar masses. The clusters are very large, with diameters measuring from 10 to as much as 300 light-years.

Most globular clusters are highly concentrated at their centres, having stellar distributions that resemble isothermal gas spheres with a cutoff that corresponds to the tidal effects of the Galaxy. A precise model of star distribution within a cluster can be derived from stellar dynamics, which takes into account the kinds of orbits that stars have in the cluster, encounters between these member stars, and the effects of exterior influences. The American astronomer Ivan R. King, for instance, derived dynamical models that fit observed stellar distributions very closely. He finds that a cluster's structure can be described in terms of two numbers: (1) the core radius, which measures the degree of concentration at the centre, and (2) the tidal radius, which measures the cut-off of star densities at the edge of the cluster.

A key distinguishing feature of globular clusters in the Galaxy is their uniformly old age. Determined by comparing the stellar population of globular clusters with stellar evolutionary models, the ages of all those so far measured range from 11 billion to 13 billion years. They are the oldest objects in the Galaxy and so must have been among the first formed. That this was the case is also indicated by the fact that the globular clusters tend to have much smaller amounts of heavy elements than do the stars in the plane of the Galaxy, e.g., the Sun.

Composed of stars belonging to the extreme Population II, as well as the high-latitude halo stars, these nearly spherical assemblages apparently formed before the material of the Milky Way Galaxy flattened into the present thin disk. As their component stars evolved, they gave up some of their gas to interstellar space. This gas was enriched in the heavy elements (i.e., elements heavier than helium) produced in stars during the later stages of their evolution, so that the interstellar gas in the Galaxy is continually being changed. Hydrogen and helium have always been the major constituents, but heavy elements have gradually grown in importance. The present interstellar gas contains elements heavier than helium at a level of about 2 percent by mass, while the globular clusters contain as little as 0.02 percent of the same elements.

OPEN CLUSTERS

Clusters smaller and less massive than the globular clusters are found in the plane of the Milky Way Galaxy intermixed with the majority of the system's stars, including the Sun. These objects are the open clusters, so called because they generally have a more open, loose appearance than typical globular clusters.

Open clusters are distributed in the Galaxy very similarly to young stars. They are highly concentrated along the plane of the Galaxy and slowly decrease in number outward from its centre. The large-scale distribution of these clusters cannot be learned directly because their existence in the Milky Way plane means that dust obscures those that are more than a few thousand light-years from the Sun. By analogy with open clusters in external galaxies similar to the Galaxy, it is surmised that they follow the general distribution of integrated light in the Milky Way Galaxy, except that there are probably fewer of them in the

Open cluster NGC 290, as seen by the Hubble Space Telescope.

central areas. There is some evidence that the younger open clusters are more densely concentrated in the Galaxy's spiral arms, at least in the neighbourhood of the Sun where these arms can be discerned.

The brightest open clusters are considerably fainter than the brightest globular clusters. The peak absolute luminosity appears to be about 50,000 times the luminosity of the Sun, but the largest percentage of known open clusters has a brightness equivalent to 500 solar luminosities. Masses can be determined from the dispersion in the measured velocities of individual stellar members of clusters. Most open clusters have small masses on the order of 50 solar masses. Their total populations of stars are small, ranging from tens to a few thousand.

Open clusters have diameters of only 2 or 3 to about 20 light-years, with the majority being less than 5 light-years across. In structure they look very different from globular clusters, though they can be understood in terms of similar dynamical models. The most important structural difference is their small total mass and relative looseness, which result from their comparatively large core radii. These two features have disastrous consequences as far as their ultimate fate is concerned, because open clusters are not sufficiently gravitationally bound to be able to withstand the disruptive tidal effects in the Galaxy. Judging from the sample of open clusters within 3,000 light-years of the Sun, only half of them can withstand such tidal forces for more than 200 million years, and a mere 2 percent have life expectancies as high as 1 billion years.

Measured ages of open clusters agree with the conclusions that have been reached about their life expectancies. They tend to be young objects; only a few are known to exceed 1 billion years in age. Most are younger than 200 million years, and some are 1 or 2 million years old. Ages of open clusters are determined by comparing their stellar membership with theoretical models of stellar evolution. Because all the stars in a cluster have very nearly the same age and chemical composition, the differences between the member stars are entirely the result of their different masses.

As time progresses after the formation of a cluster, the massive stars, which evolve the fastest, gradually disappear from the cluster, becoming white dwarf stars or other underluminous stellar remnants. Theoretical models of clusters show how this effect changes the stellar content with time, and direct comparisons with real clusters give reliable ages for them. To make this comparison, astronomers use a diagram (the colour-magnitude diagram) that plots the temperatures of the stars against their luminosities. Colour-magnitude diagrams have been obtained for more than 1,000 open clusters, and ages are thus known for this large sample.

Because open clusters are mostly young objects, they have chemical compositions that correspond to the enriched environment from which they formed. Most of them are like the Sun in their abundance of the heavy elements, and some are even richer. For instance, the Hyades, which compose one of the nearest clusters, have almost twice the abundance of heavy elements as the Sun. It became possible in the 1990s to discover very young open clusters that previously had been entirely hidden in deep, dusty regions. Using infrared array detectors, astronomers found that many molecular clouds contained very young groups of stars that had just formed and, in some cases, were still forming.

STELLAR ASSOCIATIONS

Even younger than open clusters, stellar associations are very loose groupings of young stars that share a common place and time of origin but that are not generally tied closely enough together gravitationally to form a stable cluster. Stellar associations are limited strictly to the plane of the Galaxy and appear only in regions of the system where star formation is occurring, notably in the spiral arms. They are very luminous objects. The brightest are even brighter than the brightest globular clusters, but this is not because they contain more stars; instead it is the result of the fact that their constituent stars are very much brighter than the stars constituting globular clusters.

The most luminous stars in stellar associations are very young stars of spectral types O and B. They have absolute luminosities as bright as any star in the Milky Way Galaxy—on the order of one million times the luminosity of the Sun. Such stars have very short lifetimes, only lasting a few million years. With luminous stars of this type there need not be very many to make up a highly luminous and conspicuous grouping. The total masses of stellar associations amount to only a few hundred solar masses, with the population of stars being in the hundreds or, in a few cases, thousands.

The sizes of stellar associations are large; the average diameter of those in the Galaxy is about 250 light-years. They are so large and loosely structured that their self-gravitation is insufficient to hold them together, and in a matter of a few million years the members disperse into surrounding space, becoming separate and unconnected stars in the galactic field.

MOVING GROUPS

These objects are organizations of stars that share common measurable motions. Sometimes these do not form a noticeable cluster. This definition allows the term to be applied to a range of objects from the nearest gravitationally bound clusters to groups of widely spread stars with no apparent gravitational identity, which are discovered only by searching the catalogs for stars of common motion.

Among the best known of the moving groups is the Hyades in the constellation Taurus. Also known as the Taurus moving cluster or the Taurus stream, this system comprises the relatively dense Hyades cluster along with a few very distant members. It contains a total of about 350 stars, including several white dwarfs. Its centre lies about 150 light-years away.

Other notable moving stellar groups include the Ursa

Bright nebulosity in the Pleiades (M45, NGC 1432), distance 490 light-years. Cluster stars provide the light, and surrounding clouds of dust reflect and scatter the rays from the stars.

Major, Scorpius-Centaurus, and Pleiades groups. Besides these remote organizations, investigators have observed what appear to be groups of high-velocity stars near the Sun. One of these, called the Groombridge 1830 group, consists of a number of subdwarfs and the star RR Lyrae, after which the RR Lyrae variables were named.

EMISSION NEBULAE

A conspicuous component of the Galaxy is the collection of large, bright, diffuse gaseous objects generally called nebulae. The brightest of these cloudlike objects are the emission nebulae, large complexes of interstellar gas and stars in which the gas exists in an ionized and excited state (with the electrons of the atoms excited to a higher than normal energy level). This condition is produced by the strong ultraviolet light emitted from the very luminous, hot stars embedded in the gas. Because emission nebulae consist almost entirely of ionized hydrogen, they are usually referred to as H II regions.

H II regions are found in the plane of the Milky Way Galaxy intermixed with young stars, stellar associations, and the youngest of the open clusters. They are areas where very massive stars have recently formed, and many contain the uncondensed gas, dust, and molecular complexes commonly associated with ongoing star formation. The H

II regions are concentrated in the spiral arms of the Galaxy, though some exist between the arms.

Centre of the Orion Nebula (M42).

Many of them are found at intermediate distances from the centre of the Milky Way Galaxy, with the largest number occurring at a distance of 10,000 light-years. This latter fact can be ascertained even though the H II regions cannot be seen clearly beyond a few thousand light-years from the Sun. They emit radio radiation of a characteristic type, with a thermal spectrum that indicates that their temperatures are about 10,000 kelvins. This thermal radio radiation enables astronomers to map the distribution of H II regions in distant parts of the Galaxy.

PLANETARY NEBULAE

The gaseous clouds known as planetary nebulae are only superficially similar to other types of nebulae. So called because the smaller varieties almost resemble planetary disks when viewed through a telescope, planetary nebulae represent a stage at the end of the stellar life cycle rather than one at the beginning. The distribution of such nebulae in the Galaxy is different from that of H II regions.

Planetary nebulae belong to an intermediate population and are found throughout the disk and the inner halo. There are more than 1,000 known planetary nebulae in the Milky Way Galaxy, but more might be overlooked because of obscuration in the Milky Way region.

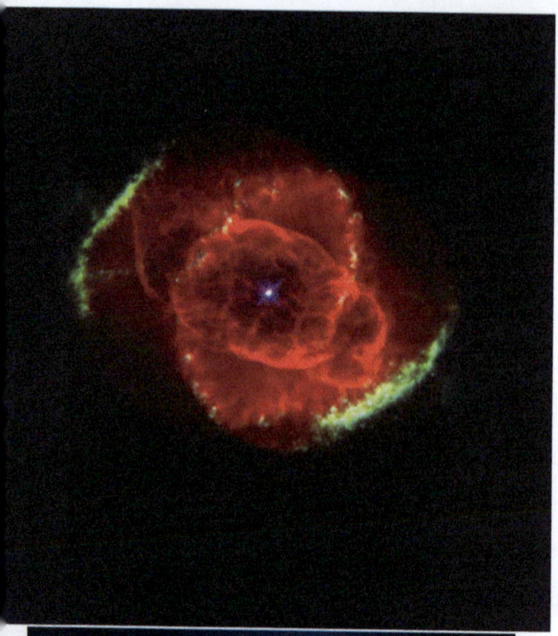

Composite image of the Cat's Eye Nebula (NGC 6543).

Another type of nebulous object found in the Galaxy is the remnant of the gas blown out from an exploding star that forms a supernova. Occasionally these objects look something like planetary nebulae, as in the case of the Crab Nebula, but they differ from the latter in three ways: (1) the total mass of their gas (they involve a larger mass, essentially all the mass of the exploding star), (2) their kinematics (they are expanding with higher velocities), and (3) their lifetimes (they last for a shorter time as visible nebulae).

The best-known supernova remnants are those resulting from three historically observed supernovae: that of 1054, which made the Crab Nebula its remnant; that of 1572, called Tycho's Nova; and that of 1604, called Kepler's Nova. These objects and the many others like them in the Galaxy are detected at radio wavelengths. They release radio energy in a nearly flat spectrum because of the emission of radiation by charged particles moving spirally at nearly the speed of light in a magnetic field enmeshed in the gaseous remnant. Radiation generated in this way is called synchrotron radiation and is associated with various types of violent cosmic phenomena besides supernova remnants, as, for example, radio galaxies.

DUST CLOUDS

The dust clouds of the Milky Way Galaxy are narrowly limited to the plane of the Milky Way, though very low-density dust can be detected even near the galactic poles. Dust clouds beyond 2,000 to 3,000 light-years from the Sun cannot be detected optically, because intervening clouds of dust and the general dust layer obscure more distant views. Based on the distribution of dust clouds in other galaxies, it can be concluded that they are often most conspicuous within the spiral arms, especially along the inner edge of well-defined ones.

The best-observed dust clouds near the Sun have masses of several hundred solar masses and sizes ranging from a maximum of about 200 light-years to a fraction of a light-year. The smallest tend to be the densest, possibly partly because of evolution: as a dust complex contracts, it also becomes denser and more opaque. The very smallest dust clouds are the so-called Bok globules, named after the Dutch American astronomer Bart J. Bok; these objects are about one light-year across and have masses of 1–20 solar masses.

More complete information on the dust in the Galaxy comes from infrared observations. While optical instruments can detect the dust when it obscures more distant objects or when it is illuminated by very nearby stars, infrared telescopes are able to register the long-wavelength radiation that the cool dust clouds themselves emit. A complete survey of the sky at infrared wavelengths made during the early 1980s by an unmanned orbiting observatory, the Infrared Astronomical Satellite (IRAS), revealed a large number of dense dust clouds in the Milky Way. Twenty years later the Spitzer Space Telescope, with greater sensitivity, greater wavelength coverage, and better resolution, mapped many dust complexes in the Milky Way. In some it was possible to view massive star clusters still in the process of formation.

The Eagle Nebula. Stars are forming in this column of cold dust and gas, which is 9.5 light-years in length.

Thick clouds of dust in the Milky Way can be studied by still another means. Many such objects contain detectable amounts of molecules that emit radio radiation at wavelengths that allow them to be identified and analyzed. More than 50 different molecules, including carbon monoxide and formaldehyde, and radicals have been detected in dust clouds.

THE INTERSTELLAR MEDIUM

The stars in the Galaxy, especially along the Milky Way, reveal the presence of a general, all-pervasive interstellar medium by the way in which they gradually fade with distance. This occurs primarily because of interstellar dust, which obscures and reddens starlight. On the average, stars near the Sun are dimmed by a factor of two for every 3,000 light-years. Thus, a star that is 6,000 light-years away in the plane of the Galaxy will appear four times fainter than it would otherwise were it not for the interstellar dust.

Another way in which the effects of interstellar dust become apparent is through the polarization of background starlight. Dust is aligned in space to some extent, and this results in selective absorption such that there is a preferred plane of vibration for the light waves. The electric vectors tend to lie preferentially along the galactic plane, though there are areas where the distribution is more complicated.

It is likely that the polarization arises because the dust grains are partially aligned by the galactic magnetic field. If the dust grains are paramagnetic so that they act somewhat like a magnet, then the general magnetic field, though very weak, can in time line up the grains with their short axes in the direction of the field. As a consequence, the directions of polarization for stars in different parts of the sky make it possible to plot the direction of the magnetic field in the Milky Way.

The dust is accompanied by gas, which is thinly dispersed among the stars, filling the space between them. This interstellar gas consists mostly of hydrogen in its neutral form. Radio telescopes can detect neutral hydrogen because it emits radiation at a wavelength of 21 cm. Such radio wavelength is long enough to penetrate interstellar dust and so can be detected from all parts of the Milky Way Galaxy.

Most of what astronomers have learned about the large-scale structure and motions of the Galaxy has been derived from the radio waves of interstellar neutral hydrogen. The distance to the gas detected is not easily determined. Statistical arguments must be used in many cases, but the velocities of the gas, when compared with the velocities found for stars and those anticipated on the basis of the dynamics of the Milky Way Galaxy, provide useful clues as to the location of the different sources of hydrogen radio emission. Near the Sun the average density of interstellar gas is 10^{-21} gm/cm^3, which is the equivalent of about one hydrogen atom per cubic centimetre.

Even before they first detected the emission from neutral hydrogen in 1951, astronomers were aware of interstellar gas. Minor components of the gas, such as sodium and calcium, absorb light at specific wavelengths, and they thus cause the appearance of absorption lines in the spectra of the stars that lie beyond the gas. Since the lines originating from stars are usually different, it is possible to distinguish the lines of the interstellar gas and to measure both the density and velocity of the gas. Frequently it is even possible to observe the effects of several concentrations of interstellar gas between Earth and the background stars and thereby determine the kinematics of the gas in different parts of the Galaxy.

COMPANIONS OF THE MILKY WAY GALAXY

The Magellanic Clouds were recognized early in the 20th century as companion objects to the Galaxy. When American astronomer Edwin Hubble established the extragalactic nature of what we now call galaxies, it became plain that the Clouds had to be separate systems, both of the irregular class and more than 100,000 light-years distant. (The current best values for their distances are 163,000 and 202,000 light-years for the Large and Small Clouds, respectively.)

Globular cluster NGC 1850 in the Large Magellanic Cloud.

Additional close companions have been found, all of them small and inconspicuous objects of the dwarf elliptical class.

The nearest of these is the Sagittarius dwarf, a galaxy that is falling into the Milky Way Galaxy, having been captured tidally by the Galaxy's much stronger gravity. The core of this galaxy is about 90,000 light-years distant. Other close companions are the well-studied Carina, Draco, Fornax, Leo I, Leo II, Sextans, Sculptor, and Ursa Minor galaxies, as well as several very faint, less well-known objects. Distances for them range from approximately 200,000 to 800,000 light-years. The grouping of these galaxies around the Galaxy is mimicked in the case of the Andromeda Galaxy, which is also accompanied by several dwarf companions.

The concept of different populations of stars has undergone considerable change over the last several decades. Before the 1940s, astronomers were aware of differences between stars and had largely accounted for most of them in terms of different masses, luminosities, and orbital characteristics around the Milky Way Galaxy. Understanding of evolutionary differences, however, had not yet been achieved, and, although differences in the chemical abundances in the stars were known, their significance was not comprehended. At this juncture, chemical differences seemed exceptional and erratic and remained uncorrelated with other stellar properties. There was still no systematic division of stars even into different kinematic families, in spite of the advances in theoretical work on the dynamics of the Galaxy.

SIZE OF THE MILKY WAY GALAXY

The first reliable measurement of the size of the Milky Way Galaxy was made in 1917 by American astronomer Harlow Shapley. He arrived at his size determination by establishing the spatial distribution of globular clusters. Shapley found that, instead of a relatively small system with the Sun near its centre, as had previously been thought, the Galaxy is immense, with the Sun nearer the edge than the centre. Assuming that the globular clusters outlined the Galaxy, he determined that it has a diameter of about 100,000 light-years and that the Sun lies about 30,000 light-years from the centre.

His values have held up remarkably well over the years. Depending in part on the particular component being discussed, the stellar disk of the Milky Way system is just about as large as Shapley's model predicted, with neutral hydrogen somewhat more widely dispersed and dark (i.e., unobservable) matter perhaps filling an even larger volume than expected. The most-distant stars and gas clouds of the system that have had their distance reliably determined lie roughly 100,000 light-years from the galactic centre, while the distance of the Sun from the centre has been found to be approximately 25,000 light-years.

The Milky Way Galaxy's structure is fairly typical of a large spiral system. This structure can be viewed as consisting of six separate parts: (1) a nucleus, (2) a central bulge, (3) a disk (both a thin and a thick disk), (4) spiral arms, (5) a spherical component, and (6) a massive halo. Some of these components blend into each other.

THE MILKY WAY GALAXY NUCLEUS

At the very centre of the Milky Way Galaxy lies a remarkable object—in all likelihood a massive black hole surrounded by an accretion disk of high-temperature gas. Neither the central object nor any of the material immediately around it can be observed at optical wavelengths because of the thick screen of intervening dust in the Milky Way. The object, however, is readily detectable at radio wavelengths and has been dubbed Sagittarius A* by radio astronomers.

The Milky Way Galaxy.

Somewhat similar to the centres of active galaxies, though on a lesser scale, the galactic nucleus is the site of a wide range of activity apparently powered by the black hole. Infrared radiation and X-rays are emitted from the area, and rapidly moving gas clouds can be observed there. Data strongly indicate that material is being pulled into the black hole from outside the nuclear region, including some gas from the z direction (i.e., perpendicular to the galactic plane). As the gas nears the black hole, the central object's strong gravitational force squeezes the gas into a rapidly rotating disk, which extends outward about 5–30 light-years from the black hole. Rotation measurements of the disk and the orbital motions of stars (seen at infrared wavelengths) indicate that the black hole has a mass more than 4,000,000 times that of the Sun.

THE CENTRAL BULGE

Surrounding the nucleus is an extended bulge of stars that is nearly spherical in shape and that consists primarily of Population II stars, though they are comparatively rich in heavy elements. Mixed with the stars are several globular

UNDERSTANDING BLACK HOLES

Black holes are regions of space that exert such powerful gravity that they suck in any matter that comes too close. That matter—whether it is a comet, a planet, or a cloud of gas—is crushed to infinite density. The gravity is so intense that it tugs at time and space, slowing down time and stretching out space. Not even light can escape the fierce gravitational pull, so the regions remain black and invisible.

Black holes seem more like science fiction than reality. But since 1916, when Albert Einstein developed his general theory of relativity, scientists have

(CONTINUED ON THE NEXT PAGE)

(CONTINUED FROM THE PREVIOUS PAGE)

known that black holes may exist, and in 1994 astronomers confirmed the existence of a black hole.

Einstein's theory suggested that if gravity could become strong enough, it would rob light of all its energy, trapping it in the same way in which it traps a planet's atmosphere. For gravity to be that strong, however, its source would have to be an extremely dense object, one with a very large mass compressed into a very small space. In 1916 the German astronomer Karl Schwarzschild calculated just how compressed a star would have to be for its gravity to trap light. According to Schwarzschild's calculations, a star the size of the Sun—864,950 miles (1,392,000 kilometers) in diameter—would have to shrink to less than 1.9 miles (3 kilometers) wide.

In 1939 the U.S. physicists J. Robert Oppenheimer and Hartland S. Snyder discovered that it is possible for stars much larger than the Sun to become this small. For most of their lives, stars remain a constant size because they contain a balance of forces: energy generated by nuclear reactions in the star's core expands the star outward, while the force of gravity pulls it in. Eventually, in billions of years, the star exhausts its nuclear fuel and collapses under its own weight. Oppenheimer and Snyder proved that if the star is more than 3.2 times as massive as the Sun, nothing can stop the collapse. Scientists believe that the Galaxy may harbor perhaps 100 million black holes left behind by collapsed stars.

Because black holes are invisible, astronomers try to locate them by observing their effects. Matter swirling toward the centre of a black hole should emit rapidly pulsating and detectable X-rays. In 1965 astronomers observed intense X-rays radiating from the constellation Cygnus, nearly 10,000 light-years away from Earth. In 1971 the world's first X-ray satellite pinpointed the exact location of these X-rays, a massive but invisible object in the binary star system Cygnus X-1—a black hole.

A supermassive black hole may form at the centre of galaxies and quasars. Some astronomers believe that these black holes form not from stars but from large volumes of interstellar gas that collect and collapse. One such supermassive black hole is found at the centre of the Galaxy. In 1990 detailed images of the centre of the galaxy showed tremendous bursts of energy emanating from its centre. In 2005 infrared observations of stars orbiting around the centre of the galaxy demonstrated the presence of a black hole there with 4.3 million times the mass of the Sun. Supermassive black holes have also been found in other galaxies, including M87.

clusters of similar stars, and both the stars and the clusters have nearly radial orbits around the nucleus. The bulge stars can be seen optically where they stick up above the obscuring dust of the galactic plane.

THE DISK

From a distance the most conspicuous part of the Milky Way Galaxy would be the disk, which extends from the nucleus out to approximately 75,000 light-years. The

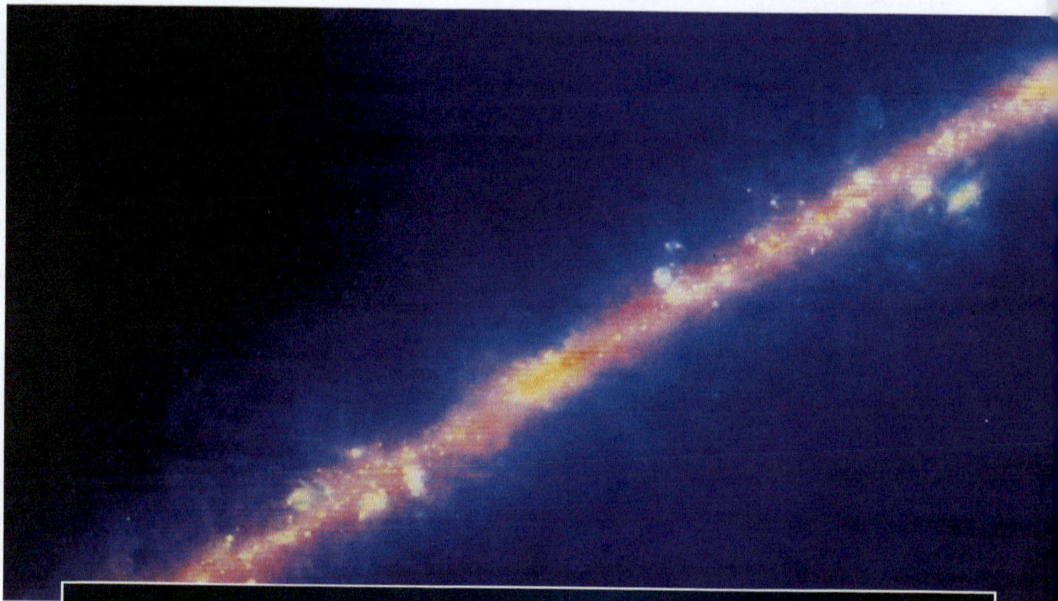

Image of the centre of the Milky Way Galaxy. The yellow and green spots and blobs are giant clouds of interstellar gas and dust. The warmest material appears blue and colder material red.

Galaxy resembles other spiral systems, featuring as it does a bright, flat arrangement of stars and gas clouds that is spread out over its entirety and marked by a spiral structure. The disk can be thought of as being the underlying body of stars upon which the arms are superimposed. This body has a thickness that is roughly one-fifth its diameter, but different components have different characteristic thicknesses. The thinnest component, often called the "thin disk," includes the dust and gas and the youngest stars, while a thicker component, the "thick disk," includes somewhat older stars.

THE SPIRAL ARMS

Astronomers did not know that the Galaxy had a spiral structure until 1953, when the distances to stellar associations were first obtained reliably. Because of the obscuring interstellar dust and the interior location of the solar system, the spiral structure is very difficult to detect optically. This structure is easier to discern from radio maps of either neutral hydrogen or molecular clouds, since both can be detected through the dust. Distances to the observed neutral hydrogen atoms must be estimated on the basis of measured velocities used in conjunction with a rotation curve for the Galaxy, which can be built up from measurements made at different galactic longitudes.

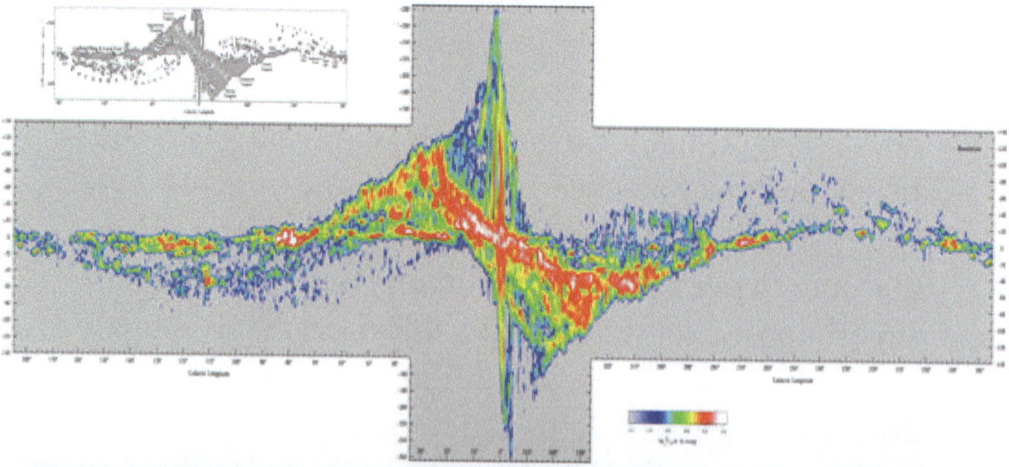

Longitude-velocity map of the Milky Way Galaxy. The vertical axis represents velocity and the horizontal axis longitude. The curves at the left and right trace the spiral arms.

Theoretical understanding of the Milky Way Galaxy's spiral arms has progressed greatly since the 1950s, but there is still no complete understanding of the relative importance of the various effects thought to determine their structure. The overall pattern is almost certainly the result of a general dynamical effect known as a density-wave pattern.

The American astronomers Chia-Chiao Lin and Frank H. Shu showed that a spiral shape is a natural result of any large-scale disturbance of the density distribution of stars in a galactic disk. When the interaction of the stars with one another is calculated, it is found that the resulting density distribution takes on a spiral pattern that does not rotate with the stars but rather moves around the nucleus more slowly as a fixed pattern. Individual stars in their orbits pass in and out of the spiral arms, slowing down in the arms temporarily and thereby causing the density enhancement. For the Galaxy, comparison of neutral hydrogen data with the calculations of Lin and Shu have shown that the pattern speed is 4 km/sec per 1,000 light-years.

Other effects that can influence a galaxy's spiral shape have been explored. It has been demonstrated, for example, that a general spiral pattern will result simply from the fact that the galaxy has differential rotation; i.e., the rotation speed is different at different distances from the galactic centre. Any disturbance, such as a sequence of stellar formation events that are sometimes found drawn out in a near-linear pattern, will eventually take on a spiral shape simply because of the differential rotation. For example, the outer spiral structure in some galaxies may be the result of tidal encounters with other galaxies or galactic cannibalism. Distortions that also can be included are the results of massive explosions such as supernova events. These, however, tend to have only fairly local effects.

THE SPHERICAL COMPONENT

The space above and below the disk of the Galaxy is occupied by a thinly populated extension of the central bulge. Nearly spherical in shape, this region is populated by the outer globular clusters, but it also contains many individual field stars of extreme Population II, such as RR Lyrae variables and dwarf stars deficient in the heavy elements. Structurally, the spherical component resembles an elliptical galaxy, following the same simple mathematical law of how density varies with distance from the centre.

THE MILKY WAY GALAXY'S MASSIVE HALO

The least-understood component of the Milky Way Galaxy is the giant massive halo that is exterior to the entire visible part. The existence of the massive halo is demonstrated by its effect on the outer rotation curve of the Galaxy. All that can be said with any certainty is that the halo extends considerably beyond a distance of 100,000 light-years from the centre and that its mass is several times greater than the mass of the rest of the Galaxy taken together. It is not known what its shape is, what its constituents are, or how far into intergalactic space it extends.

MAGNETIC FIELD

It was once thought that the spiral structure of galaxies might be controlled by a strong magnetic field. However, when the general magnetic field was detected by radio techniques, it was found to be too weak to have large-scale effects on galactic structure. The strength of the galactic field is only about 0.000001 times the strength of Earth's field at its surface, a value that is much too low to have dynamical effects on the interstellar gas that could account for the order represented by the spiral-arm structure. This is, however, sufficient strength to cause a general alignment of the dust grains in interstellar space, a feature that is detected by measurements of the polarization of starlight. In the prevailing model of interstellar dust grains, the particles are shown to be rapidly spinning and to contain small amounts of metal (probably iron), though the primary constituents are ice and carbon. The magnetic field of the Milky Way Galaxy can gradually act on the dust particles and cause their rotational axes to line up in such a way that their short axes are parallel to the direction of the field. The field itself is aligned along the Milky Way band, so that the short axes of the particles also become aligned along the galactic plane. Polarization measurements of stars at low galactic latitudes confirm this pattern.

ROTATION OF THE MILKY WAY GALAXY

The motions of stars in the local stellar neighbourhood can be understood in terms of a general population of stars that have circular orbits of rotation around the distant galactic nucleus, with an admixture of stars that have more highly elliptical orbits and that appear to be high-velocity stars to a terrestrial observer as Earth moves with the Sun in its circular orbit. The general rotation of the disk stars was first detected through studies made in the 1920s, notably those of the Swedish astronomer Bertil Lindblad, who correctly interpreted the apparent asymmetries in stellar motions as the result of this multiple nature of stellar orbital characteristics.

The disk component of the Galaxy rotates around the nucleus in a manner similar to the pattern for the planets of the solar system, which have nearly circular orbits around the Sun. Because the rotation rate is different at different distances from the centre of the Milky Way Galaxy, the measured velocities of disk stars in different directions along the Milky Way exhibit different patterns. The Dutch astronomer Jan H. Oort first interpreted this effect in terms of galactic rotation motions, employing the radial velocities and proper motions of stars. He demonstrated that differential rotation leads to a systematic variation of the radial velocities of stars with galactic longitude following the mathematical expression:

$$\text{radial velocity} = Ar \sin 2l$$

where A is called Oort's constant and is approximately 15 km/sec/kiloparsec (1 kiloparsec is 3,260 light-years), r is the distance to the star, and *l* is the galactic longitude.

A similar expression can be derived for measured proper motions of stars. The agreement of observed data with Oort's formulas was a landmark demonstration of the correctness of Lindblad's ideas about stellar motions. It led to the modern understanding of the Galaxy as consisting of a giant rotating disk with other, more spherical, and more slowly rotating components superimposed.

THE GALAXY'S MASS

The total mass of the Milky Way Galaxy, which had seemed reasonably well established during the 1960s, has become a matter of considerable uncertainty. Measuring the mass out to the distance of the farthest large hydrogen clouds is a relatively straightforward procedure. The measurements required are the velocities and positions of neutral hydrogen gas, combined with the approximation that the gas is rotating in nearly circular orbits around the centre of the Galaxy. A rotation curve, which relates the circular velocity of the gas to its distance from the galactic centre, is constructed. The shape of this curve and its values are determined by the amount of gravitational pull that the Galaxy exerts on the gas. Velocities are low in the central parts of the system because not much mass is interior to the orbit of the gas; most of the Galaxy is exterior to it and

does not exert an inward gravitational pull. Velocities are high at intermediate distances because most of the mass in that case is inside the orbit of the gas clouds and the gravitational pull inward is at a maximum. At the farthest distances, the velocities decrease because nearly all the mass is interior to the clouds.

This portion of the Galaxy is said to have Keplerian orbits, since the material should move in the same manner that the German astronomer Johannes Kepler discovered the planets to move within the solar system, where virtually all the mass is concentrated inside the orbits of the orbiting bodies. The total mass of the Galaxy is then found by constructing mathematical models of the system with different amounts of material distributed in various ways and by comparing the resulting velocity curves with the observed one. As applied in the 1960s, this procedure indicated that the total mass of the Milky Way Galaxy was approximately 200 billion times the mass of the Sun.

During the 1980s, however, refinements in the determination of the velocity curve began to cast doubts on the earlier results. The downward trend to lower velocities in the outer parts of the Galaxy was found to have been in error. Instead, the curve remained almost constant,

Large Magellanic Cloud. The bright nebula at the top of the image is 30 Doradus, also known as the Tarantula Nebula.

indicating that there continue to be substantial amounts of matter exterior to the measured hydrogen gas. This in turn indicates that there must be some undetected material out there that is completely unexpected. It must extend considerably beyond the previously accepted positions of the edge of the Galaxy, and it must be dark at virtually all wavelengths, as it remains undetected even when searched for with radio, X-ray, ultraviolet, infrared, and optical telescopes. Until the dark matter is identified and its distribution determined, it will be impossible to measure the total mass of the Galaxy, so all that can be said is that the mass is at least several hundred billion, and possibly one trillion, times the mass of the Sun.

The nature of the dark matter in the Galaxy remains one of the major questions of galactic astronomy. Many other galaxies also appear to have such undetected matter. In the 1990s astronomers carried out exhaustive lensing experiments involving the study of millions of stars in the galactic central areas and in the Magellanic Clouds to search for dark objects whose masses would cause lensed brightenings of background stars. Some lensing events were detected, but the number of dark objects inferred is not enough to explain completely the dark matter in galaxies and galaxy clusters. It is likely that the dark matter consists of some undiscovered particle, such as a WIMP (weakly interacting massive particle).

CHAPTER 2

THE STUDY OF GALAXIES

Just as the Sun is one of many stars in the Milky Way Galaxy, the Milky Way Galaxy is just one of many galaxies in the universe. The latest estimate is that there are about 2 trillion galaxies. Nature has provided an immensely varied array of galaxies, ranging from faint, diffuse dwarf objects to brilliant spiral-shaped giants. Virtually all galaxies appear to have been formed soon after the universe began, and they pervade space, even into the depths of the farthest reaches penetrated by powerful modern telescopes. Galaxies usually exist in clusters, some of which in turn are grouped into larger clusters that measure hundreds of millions of light-years across. These so-called superclusters are separated by nearly empty voids, and this causes the gross structure of the universe to look somewhat like a network of sheets and chains of galaxies.

Galaxies differ from one another in shape, with variations resulting from the way in which the systems were formed and subsequently evolved. Galaxies are extremely varied not

The Whirlpool Galaxy (*left*), also known as M51, an Sc galaxy accompanied by a small irregular companion galaxy, NGC 5195 (*right*).

only in structure but also in the amount of activity observed. Some are sites of vigorous star formation, with its attendant glowing gas and clouds of dust and molecular complexes. Others, by contrast, are quiescent, having long ago ceased to form new stars. Perhaps the most conspicuous activity in galaxies occurs in their nuclei, where evidence suggests that in many cases supermassive objects—probably black holes—lurk. These central black holes apparently formed several billion years ago; they are now observed forming in galaxies at large distances (and, therefore, because of the time it takes light to travel to Earth, at times in the far distant past) as brilliant objects called quasars.

The existence of galaxies was not recognized until the early 20th century. Since then, however, galaxies have become one of the focal points of astronomical investigation. The notable developments and achievements in the study of galaxies are surveyed here. Included in the discussion are the external galaxies (i.e., those lying outside the Galaxy, the local galaxy to which the Sun and Earth belong), their distribution in clusters and superclusters, and the evolution of galaxies and quasars.

GALAXY EVOLUTION

The study of the origin and evolution of galaxies and the quasar phenomenon has only just begun. Many models of galaxy formation and evolution have been constructed on the basis of what we know about conditions in the early universe, which is in turn based on models of the expansion of the universe after the big bang (the primordial explosion from which the universe is thought to have originated) and on the characteristics of the cosmic microwave background (the observed photons that show us the light-filled universe as it was when it was a few hundred thousand years old).

According to the big-bang model, the universe expanded rapidly from a highly compressed primordial state, which resulted in a significant decrease in density and temperature. Soon afterward, the dominance of matter over antimatter (as observed today) may have been established by processes that also predict proton decay. During this stage many types of elementary particles may have been present. After a few seconds, the universe cooled enough to allow the formation of certain nuclei. The theory predicts that definite amounts of hydrogen, helium, and lithium were produced. Their abundances agree with what is observed today. About one million years later the universe was sufficiently cool for atoms to form.

When the universe had expanded to be cool enough for matter to remain in neutral atoms without being instantly ionized by radiation, structure apparently had already been established in the form of density fluctuations. At a crucial point in time, there condensed from the expanding matter small clouds (protogalaxies) that could collapse under their own gravitational field eventually to form galaxies.

For the latter half of the 20th century, there were two competing models of galaxy formation: "top-down" and "bottom-up." In the top-down model, galaxies formed out of the collapse of much larger gas clouds. In the bottom-up model, galaxies formed from the merger of smaller entities that were the size of globular clusters. In both models the angular momentum of the original clouds determined the form of the galaxy that eventually evolved. It is thought that a protogalaxy with a large amount of angular momentum tended to form a flat, rapidly rotating system (a spiral galaxy), whereas one with very little angular momentum developed into a more nearly spherical system (an elliptical galaxy).

The transition from the 20th to the 21st century coincided with a dramatic transition in our understanding of the evolution of galaxies. It is no longer believed that galaxies have evolved smoothly and alone. Indeed, it has become clear that collisions between galaxies have occurred all during their evolution—and these collisions, far from being rare events, were the mechanism by which galaxies developed in the distant past and are the means by which they are changing their structure and appearance even now. Evidence for this new understanding of galactic evolution comes primarily from two sources: more detailed studies of nearby galaxies with new, more sensitive instruments and deep surveys of extremely distant galaxies, seen when the universe was young.

Recent surveys of nearby galaxies, including the Milky Way Galaxy, have shown evidence of past collisions and capture of galaxies. For the Milky Way the most conspicuous example is the Sagittarius Galaxy, which has been absorbed by our Galaxy. Now its stars lie spread out across the sky, its seven globular clusters intermingling with the globular clusters of the Galaxy. Long tails of stars around the Milky Way were formed by the encounter and act as clues to the geometry of the event. A second remnant galaxy, known as the Canis Major Dwarf Galaxy, can also be traced by the detection of star streams in the outer parts of our Galaxy. These galaxies support the idea that the Galaxy is a mix of pieces, formed by the amalgamation of many smaller galaxies.

The Andromeda Galaxy (M31) also has a past involving collisions and accretion. Its peculiar close companion, M32, shows a structure that indicates that it was formerly a normal, more massive galaxy that lost much of its outer parts and possibly all of its globular clusters to M31 in a past encounter. Deep surveys of the outer parts of the Andromeda Galaxy have revealed huge coherent structures of star streams and clouds, with properties indicating that these include the outer remnants of smaller galaxies "eaten" by the giant central galaxy, as well as clouds of M31 stars ejected by the strong tidal forces of the collision.

More spectacular are galaxies presently in the process of collision and accretion in the more distant, but still nearby, universe. The symptoms of the collision are the distortion of the galaxies' shape (especially that of the spiral arms), the formation of giant arcs of stars by tidal action, and the enhanced rate of star and star cluster formation. Some of the most massive and luminous young star clusters observed anywhere lie in the regions where two galaxies have come together, with their gas and dust clouds colliding and merging in a spectacular cosmic reworks display.

A second type of evidence for the fact that galaxies grow by merging comes from very deep surveys of the very distant universe, especially those carried out with the Hubble Space Telescope (HST). These surveys, especially the Hubble Deep Field and the Hubble Ultra Deep Field, found galaxies so far away that the light observed by the HST left them when they were very young, only a few hundred million years old. This enables the direct detection and measurement of young galaxies as they were when the universe was young. The result is a view of a very different universe of galaxies. Instead of giant elliptical galaxies and grand spirals, the universe in its early years was populated with small, irregular objects that looked like mere fragments. These were the building blocks that eventually formed bigger galaxies such as the Milky Way. Many show active formation of stars that are deficient in heavy elements because many of the heavy elements had not yet been created when these stars were formed.

The rate of star formation in these early times was significant, but it did not reach a peak until about one billion years later. Galaxies from this time show a maximum in the amount of excited hydrogen, which indicates a high rate of star formation, as young, very hot stars are necessary for exciting interstellar hydrogen so that it can be detected. Since that time, so much matter has been locked up in stars (especially white dwarfs) that not enough interstellar dust and gas are available to achieve such high rates of star formation.

An important development that has helped our understanding of the way galaxies form is the great success of computer simulations. High-speed calculations of the gravitational history of assemblages of stars, interstellar matter, and dark matter suggest that after the big bang the universe developed as a networklike arrangement of material, with gradual condensation of masses where the strands of the network intersected. In simulations of this process, massive galaxies form, but each is surrounded by a hundred or so smaller objects. The small objects may correspond to the dwarf galaxies, such as those that surround the Galaxy but of which only a dozen or so remain, the rest having presumably been accreted by the main galaxy. Such computer models, called "n-body simulations," are especially successful in mimicking galaxy collisions and in helping to explain the presence of various tidal arms and jets observed by astronomers.

In summary, the current view of galactic history is that present-day galaxies are a mix of giant objects that accreted lesser galaxies in their vicinities, especially early in the formation of the universe, together with some remnant lesser, or dwarf, galaxies that have not yet come close enough to a more massive galaxy to be captured. The expansion of the universe gradually decreases the likelihood of such captures, so some of the dwarfs may survive to old age—eventually dying, like their giant cousins, when all of their stars become dim white dwarfs or black holes and slowly disappear.

ANDROMEDA NEBULA NOVAE

An unfortunate misidentification hampered the early recognition of the northern sky's brightest nearby galaxy, the Andromeda Nebula, also known as M31. In 1885 a bright star, previously invisible, appeared near the centre of M31, becoming almost bright enough to be seen without a telescope. As it slowly faded again, astronomers decided that it must be a nova, a "new star," similar to the class of temporary stars found relatively frequently in populous parts of the Milky Way Galaxy. If this was the case, it was argued, then its extraordinary brightness must indicate that M31 cannot be very far away, certainly not outside the local system of stars. Designated S Andromeda in conformity with the pattern of terminology applied to stars of variable brightness, this supposed nova was a strong argument in favour of the hypothesis that nebulae are nearby objects in the Galaxy.

By 1910, however, there was evidence that S Andromeda might have been wrongly identified. Deep photographs were being taken of M31 with the Mount Wilson Observatory's newly completed 152-cm (60-inch) telescope, and the astronomers at the observatory, especially J.C. Duncan and George W. Ritchey, were finding faint objects, just resolved by the longest exposures, that also seemed to behave like novae. These objects, however, were about 10,000 times fainter than S Andromeda. If they were ordinary novae, then M31 must be millions of light-years away, but then the nature of S Andromeda became a difficult question. At this vast distance its total luminosity would have to be immense—an incomprehensible output of energy for a single star.

Completion of the 254-cm (100-inch) telescope on Mount Wilson in 1917 resulted in a new series of photographs that captured even fainter objects. More novae were found in M31, mainly by Milton L. Humason, who was an assistant at the time to Edwin P. Hubble, one of the truly outstanding astronomers of the day. Hubble eventually studied 63 of these stars, and his findings proved to be one of the final solutions to the controversy.

VAN MAANEN ROTATION

During the early 20th century, one of the most important branches of astronomy was astrometry, the precise measurements of stellar positions and motions. Van Maanen was one of the leading experts in this field. Most of his determinations of stellar positions were accurate and have stood the test of time, but he made one serious and still poorly understood error when he pursued a problem tangential to his main interests. In a series of papers published in the early 1920s, van Maanen reported on his discovery and measurement of the rotation of spiral nebulae. Using early plates taken by others at the 152-cm (60-inch) Mount Wilson telescope as well as more recent ones taken about 10 years later, van Maanen measured the positions of several knotlike, nearly stellar images in the spiral arms of some of the largest-known spiral nebulae (e.g., M33, M101, and M51). Comparing the positions, he found distinct changes indicative of a rotation of the spiral pattern against the background of surrounding field stars. In each case, rotation occurs in the sense that the spiral arms trail. The periods of rotation were all approximately 100,000 years. Angular motions were about 0.02 second of arc per year.

Shapley seized the van Maanen results as evidence that the spirals had to be nearby; otherwise, their true space velocities of rotation would have to be impossibly large. For example, if M51 is rotating at an apparent rate of 0.02 second of arc per year, its true velocity would be immense if it is a distant galaxy. Assuming that a distance of 10,000,000 light-years would lead to an implausibly large rotation velocity of 12,000 km/sec (7,456 miles/sec), Shapley argued that, if a more reasonable velocity was adopted—say, 100 km/sec (62 miles/sec)—then the distances would all be less than 100,000 light-years, which would put all the spirals well within the Galaxy.

It is unclear just why such a crucial measurement went wrong. Van Maanen repeated the measures and obtained the same answer even after Hubble demonstrated the truth about the distances to the spirals. However, subsequent workers, using the same plates, failed to find any rotation. Among the various hypotheses that science historians have proposed as an explanation for the error are two particularly reasonable ideas: (1) possibly the fact that spiral nebulae look like they are rotating (i.e., they resemble familiar rotational patterns that are perceivable in nature) may have influenced the observer subconsciously, and this subtle effect manifested itself in prejudicing the delicate measurements, or (2) possibly the first set of plates was the problem. Many of these plates had been taken in an unconventional manner by Ritchey, who swung the plate holder out of the field whenever the quality of the images was temporarily poor because of atmospheric turbulence. The resulting plates appeared excellent, having been exposed only during times of very fine seeing; however, according to some interpretations, the images had a slight asymmetry that led to a very small displacement of star images compared with nonstellar images. Such an error could look like rotation if not recognized for what it really was. In any case, the van Maanen rotation was accepted by many astronomers, including Shapley, and temporarily sidetracked progress toward recognizing the truth about galaxies.

SHAPLEY-CURTIS DEBATE

The nature of galaxies and scale of the universe were the subject of the Great Debate, a public program arranged in 1920 by the National Academy of Sciences at the Smithsonian Institution in Washington, D.C. Featured were talks by Shapley and Heber Curtis, who were recognized as spokesmen for opposite views on the nature of spiral nebulae and the Milky Way Galaxy. This so-called debate has often been cited as an illustration of how revolutionary new concepts are assimilated by science. It is sometimes compared to the debate, centuries before, over the motions of the Earth (the Copernican revolution); however, though as a focal point the debate about Earth's motion can be used to define the modern controversy, the Shapley-Curtis debate actually was much more complicated.

A careful reading of the documents involved suggests that, on the broader topic of the scale of the universe, both men were making incorrect conclusions but for the same reasons—namely, for being unable to accept and comprehend the incredibly large scale of things. Shapley correctly argued for an enormous Milky Way Galaxy on the basis of the P-L (period-luminosity) relation and the globular clusters, while Curtis incorrectly rejected these lines of evidence, advocating instead a small galactic system. The P-L relation was discovered by Henrietta Leavitt of the Harvard College Observatory. In 1912 Leavitt had found that there was a close correlation between the periods of pulsation (variations in light) and the luminosities (intrinsic, or absolute, brightnesses) of a class of stars called Cepheid variables in the Small Magellanic Cloud.

Given a Milky Way Galaxy system of limited scale, Curtis could argue for and consider plausible the extragalactic nature of the spiral nebulae. Shapley, on the other hand, incorrectly rejected the island universe theory of the spirals (i.e., the hypothesis that there existed comparable galaxies beyond the boundaries of the Galaxy) because he felt that such objects would surely be engulfed by the local galactic system. Furthermore, he put aside the apparent faint novae in M31, preferring to interpret S Andromeda as an ordinary nova, for otherwise that object would have been unbelievably luminous. Unfortunately for him, such phenomena—called supernovae—do in fact exist, as was realized a few years later. Curtis was willing to concede that there might be two classes of novae, yet, because he considered the Galaxy to be small, he underestimated their differences. The van Maanen rotation also entered into Shapley's arguments: if spiral nebulae were rotating so fast, they must be within the Galaxy as he conceived it. For Curtis, however, the matter provided less of a problem: even if spiral nebulae did rotate as rapidly as claimed, the small scale of Curtis's universe allowed them to have physically reasonable speeds.

The Shapley-Curtis debate took place near the end of the era of the single-galaxy universe. In just a few years the scientific world became convinced that Shapley's grand scale of the Milky Way Galaxy was correct and at the same time that Curtis was right about the nature of spiral nebulae. Such objects indeed lie even outside Shapley's enormous Milky Way Galaxy, and they range far beyond the distances that in 1920 seemed too vast for many astronomers to comprehend.

HUBBLE AND THE DISCOVERY OF EXTRAGALACTIC OBJECTS

During the early 1920s Hubble detected 15 stars in the small, irregular cloudlike object NGC 6822 that varied in luminosity, and he suspected that they might include Cepheids. After considerable effort, he determined that 11 of them were in fact Cepheid variables, with properties indistinguishable from those of normal Cepheids in the Milky Way Galaxy and in the Magellanic Clouds. Their periods ranged from 12 to 64 days, and they were all very

Nearby irregular galaxy NGC 6822, located 1.6 million light-years from Earth, as seen in an optical image.

faint, much fainter than their Magellanic counterparts. Nevertheless, they fit a P-L relation of the same nature as had been discovered by Leavitt.

Hubble then boldly assumed that the P-L relation was universal and derived an estimate for the distance to NGC 6822, using Shapley's most recent (1925) version of the calibration of the relation. This calibration was wrong, as is now known, because of the confusion at that time over the nature of Cepheids. Shapley's calibration included certain Cepheids in globular clusters that subsequent investigators found to have their own fainter P-L relation. (Such Cepheids have been designated Type II Cepheids to distinguish them from the normal variety, which are referred to as Type I.) Thus, Hubble's distance for NGC 6822 was too small: he calculated a distance of only 700,000 light-years. Today it is recognized that the actual distance is closer to 2,000,000 light-years.

In any case, this vast distance—even though underestimated—was large enough to convince Hubble that NGC 6822 must be a remote, separate galaxy, much too far away to be included even in Shapley's version of the Galaxy system. Technically, then, this faint nebula can be considered the first recognized external galaxy. The Magellanic Clouds continued to be regarded simply as appendages to the Galaxy, and the other bright nebulae, M31 and M33, were still being studied at the Mount Wilson Observatory. Although Hubble announced his discovery of Cepheids in M31 at a meeting in 1924, he did not complete his research and publish the results for this conspicuous spiral galaxy until five years later.

While the Cepheids made it possible to determine the distance and nature of NGC 6822, some of its other features corroborated the conclusion that it was a separate, distant galaxy. Hubble discovered within it five diffuse nebulae, which are glowing gaseous clouds composed mostly of ionized hydrogen, designated H II regions. (H stands for hydrogen and II indicates that most of it is ionized; H I, by contrast, signifies neutral hydrogen.) He found that these five H II regions had spectra like those of gas clouds in the Galaxy system—e.g., the Orion Nebula and Eta Carinae. Calculating their diameters, Hubble ascertained that the sizes of the diffuse nebulae were normal, similar to those of local examples of giant H II regions. Five other diffuse objects discerned by Hubble were definitely not gaseous nebulae. He compared them with globular clusters (both in the Milky Way Galaxy and in the Magellanic Clouds) and concluded that they were too small and faint to be normal globular clusters. Convinced that they were most likely distant galaxies seen through NGC 6822, he dismissed them from further consideration. Modern studies suggest that Hubble was too hasty. Though probably not true giant globular clusters, these objects are in all likelihood star clusters in the system, fainter, smaller in population, and probably somewhat younger than normal globular clusters.

The Dutch astronomer Jacobus Cornelius Kapteyn showed in the early 20th century that statistical techniques could be used to determine the stellar luminosity function for the solar neighbourhood. (The luminosity function is a curve that shows how many stars there are in a given volume for each different stellar luminosity.) Eager to test the nature of NGC 6822, Hubble counted stars in the galaxy to various brightness limits and found a luminosity function for its brightest stars. When he compared it with Kapteyn's, the agreement was excellent—another indication that the Cepheids had given about the right distance and that the basic properties of galaxies were fairly uniform. Step by step, Hubble and his contemporaries piled up evidence for the fundamental assumption that has since guided the astronomy of the extragalactic universe, the uniformity of nature. By its bold application, astronomers have moved from a limiting one-galaxy universe to an immense vastness of space populated by trillions of galaxies, all grander in size and design than the Milky Way Galaxy system was once thought to be.

THE DISTANCE TO THE ANDROMEDA NEBULA

In 1929 Hubble published his epochal paper on M31, the great Andromeda Nebula. Based on 350 photographic plates taken at Mount Wilson, his study provided evidence that M31 is a giant stellar system like the Milky Way Galaxy.

Because M31 is much larger than the field of view of the 152- and 254-cm (60- and 100-inch) telescopes at Mount Wilson, Hubble concentrated on four regions,

EDWIN POWELL HUBBLE

U.S. astronomer Edwin Powell Hubble (1889–1953) played a crucial role in establishing the field of extragalactic astronomy—the study of objects outside the Milky Way Galaxy. He is generally regarded as the leading astronomer of the 20th century. The Hubble Space Telescope was named after him.

Hubble was born in Marshfield, Missouri, on November 20, 1889. In 1910 he graduated from the University of Chicago and was selected as a Rhodes Scholar. He spent three years at the University of Oxford and was awarded a B.A. in jurisprudence, a subject he had taken at the insistence of his father. After his father's death in 1913, the way was open for him to pursue a scientific career. He returned to the United States and began graduate studies in astronomy at the University of Chicago.

After serving in the U.S. Army during World War I, Hubble earned his doctorate and went to work with his former teacher, George Hale, at the Mount Wilson Observatory in California. There he observed spiral nebulas, objects he had investigated for his doctorate. The status of these objects was then unclear. It was unknown whether they were distant star systems comparable to the Milky Way Galaxy or clouds of gas or sparse star clusters within, or close by, the Milky Way.

In 1923 Hubble found a type of star called Cepheid variables in the Andromeda Nebula, a very well-known spiral. He used the fluctuations in light of these stars to determine the nebula's distance. He determined that the nebula was several hundred thousand light-years away (outside the Milky Way Galaxy) and that it was actually another galaxy. Hubble's finds in the Andromeda Nebula and in other relatively nearby spiral nebulae swiftly convinced the great majority of astronomers that the universe in fact contains many galaxies.

In studying those galaxies in 1927 Hubble made his second remarkable discovery: that the galaxies were receding from the Milky Way at rates that increased with distance. This implied that the universe, long considered unchanging, was expanding. Even more remarkable, the ratio of the galaxies' speed to their distance was a constant, named Hubble's constant in his honor. Hubble's original calculation of the constant was incorrect: it made the Milky Way larger than all other galaxies and the entire universe younger than the surmised age of Earth. Later astronomers determined that galaxies were systematically more distant, resolving the discrepancy. Hubble died in San Marino, California, on September 28, 1953.

centred on the nucleus and at various distances along the major axis. The total area studied amounted to less than half the galaxy's size, and the other unexplored regions remained largely unknown for 50 years. (Modern comprehensive optical studies of M31 have been conducted only since about 1980.)

Hubble pointed out an important and puzzling feature of the resolvability of M31. Its central regions, including the nucleus and diffuse nuclear bulge, were not well resolved into stars, one reason that the true nature of M31 had previously been elusive. However, the outer parts along the spiral arms in particular were resolved into swarms of faint stars, seen superimposed over a structured background of light. Current understanding of this fact is that spiral galaxies typically have central bulges made up exclusively of very old stars, the brightest of which are too faint to be visible on Hubble's plates. Not until 1944 did the German-born astronomer Walter Baade finally resolve the bulge of M31. Using red-sensitive plates and very long exposures, he managed to detect the brightest red giants of this old population. Out in the arms there exist many young, bright, hot blue stars, and these are easily resolved. The brightest are so luminous that they can be seen even with moderate-sized telescopes.

The most important of Hubble's discoveries was that of M31's population of Cepheid variables. Forty of the 50 variables detected turned out to be ordinary Cepheids with periods ranging from 10 to 48 days. A clear relation was found between their periods and luminosities, and the slope of the relation agreed with those for the Magellanic Clouds and NGC 6822. Hubble's comparison indicated that M31 must be 8.5 times more distant than the Small Magellanic Cloud (SMC), which would imply a distance of two million light-years if the modern SMC distance was used (the 1929 value employed by Hubble was about two times too small). Clearly, M31 must be a distant, large galaxy.

Other features announced in Hubble's paper were M31's population of bright, irregular, slowly varying variables. One of the irregulars was exceedingly bright; it is among the most luminous stars in the galaxy and is a prototype of a class of high-luminosity stars now called Hubble-Sandage variables, which are found in many giant galaxies. Eighty-five novae, all behaving very much like those in the Milky Way Galaxy, were also analyzed. Hubble estimated that the true occurrence rate of novae in M31 must be about 30 per year, a figure that was later confirmed by the American astronomer Halton C. Arp in a systematic search.

Hubble found numerous star clusters in M31, especially globular clusters, 140 of which he eventually cataloged. He clinched the argument that M31 was a galaxy similar to the Milky Way Galaxy by calculating its mass and mass density. Using the velocities that had been measured for the inner parts of M31 by spectrographic work, he calculated (on the basis of the distance derived from the Cepheids) that M31's mass must be about 3.5 billion times that of the Sun. Today astronomers have much better data, which indicate that the galaxy's true total mass must be at least 100 times greater than Hubble's value, but even that value clearly showed that M31 is an immense system of stars. Furthermore, Hubble's estimates of star densities demonstrated that the stars in the outer arm areas of M31 are spread out with about the same density as in the Milky Way Galaxy system in the vicinity of the Sun.

EXTRAGALACTIC ASTRONOMY

Until about 1950, scientific knowledge of galaxies advanced slowly. Only a very small number of astronomers took up galaxy studies, and only a very few telescopes were suitable for significant research. It was an exclusive field, rather jealously guarded by its practitioners, and so progress was orderly but limited.

During the decade of the 1950s, the field began to change. Ever-larger optical telescopes became available, and the space program resulted in a sizable increase in the number of astronomers emerging from universities. New instrumentation enabled investigators to explore galaxies in entirely new ways, making it possible to detect

Spiral galaxy M81 (*bottom*) and irregular galaxy M82 (*top*), as seen in ultraviolet light by the Galaxy Evolution Explorer (GALEX) satellite.

their radio, infrared, and ultraviolet emissions and eventually even radiation at X-ray and gamma-ray wavelengths.

Today, galaxies are being extensively studied with giant arrays of ground-based radio telescopes, Earth-orbiting optical, X-ray, ultraviolet, and infrared telescopes, and high-speed computers. Studies that have given rise to remarkable advances in knowledge and understanding. The tremendous progress in both theoretical and observational work has led many to say that the turn of the 21st century happened during the "golden age" of extragalactic astronomy.

CHAPTER 3

Galaxies of Many Types

Astronomers classify galaxies into three main types according to their appearance: elliptical, spiral, and irregular. Elliptical galaxies range in shape from nearly spherical to very flattened and round or oval. A large fraction of the bright galaxies in the sky are spiral galaxies, which are shaped like pinwheels, having a fairly flat main disk with spiral arms winding out from the centre. A spiral system has a central bulge and tapers gradually toward the outer edges. The arms contain the greatest concentration of the galaxy's interstellar gas and dust, where stars can form. Unlike elliptical and spiral galaxies, irregular galaxies do not have a symmetrical shape, and they lack an obvious nucleus. These unusually shaped galaxies are not very common.

Almost all current systems of galaxy classification are outgrowths of the initial scheme proposed by Edwin Hubble in 1926. Hubble subdivided ellipticals, spirals, and irregulars into finer groups.

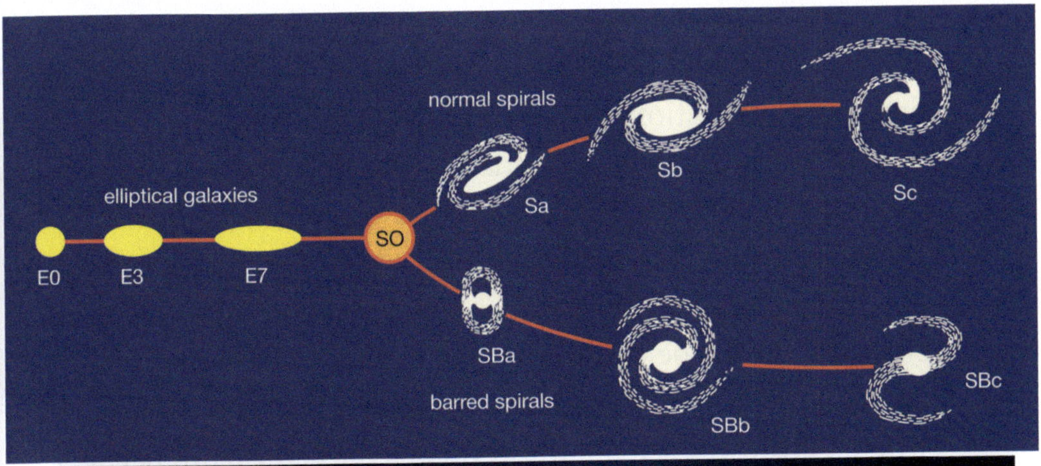

Hubble's system of classification for galaxies.

In *The Hubble Atlas of Galaxies* (1961), the American astronomer Allan R. Sandage drew on Hubble's notes and his own research on galaxy morphology to revise the Hubble classification scheme. Some of the features of this revised scheme are subject to argument because of the findings of very recent research, but its general features, especially the coding of types, remain viable. A description of the classes as defined by Sandage is given here, along with observations concerning needed refinements of some of the details.

ELLIPTICAL GALAXIES

These systems exhibit certain characteristic properties. They have complete rotational symmetry; i.e., they are figures of revolution with two equal principal axes. They have a third smaller axis that is the presumed axis of rotation. The surface brightness of ellipticals at optical wavelengths decreases monotonically outward from a maximum value at the centre, following a common mathematical law of the form:

$$I = I_0(r/a +1)^{-2}$$

where I is the intensity of the light, I_0 is the central intensity, r is the radius, and a is a scale factor. The isophotal contours exhibited by an elliptical system are similar ellipses with a common orientation, each centred on its nucleus. No galaxy of this type is flatter than $b/a = 0.3$, with b and a the minor and major axes of the elliptical image, respectively. Ellipticals contain neither interstellar dust nor bright stars of spectral types O and B. Many, however, contain evidence of the presence of low-density gas in their nuclear regions. Ellipticals are red in colour, and their spectra indicate that their light comes mostly from old stars, especially evolved red giants.

Subclasses of elliptical galaxies are defined by their apparent shape, which is of course not necessarily their three-dimensional shape. The designation is E*n*, where n is an integer defined by

$$n = 10(a- b)/a.$$

A perfectly circular image will be an E0 galaxy, while a flatter object might be an E7 galaxy. (Elliptical galaxies are never flatter than this, so there are no E8, E9, or E10 galaxies.)

Although the above-cited criteria are generally accepted, current high-quality measurements have shown that some significant deviations exist. Most elliptical galaxies do not, for instance, exactly fit the intensity law formulated by Hubble; deviations are evident in their innermost parts and in their faint outer parts. Furthermore, many elliptical galaxies have slowly varying ellipticity, with the images being more circular in the central regions than in the outer parts. The major axes sometimes do not line up either; their position angles vary in the outer parts. Finally, astronomers have found that a few ellipticals do in fact have small numbers of luminous O and B stars as well as dust lanes.

SPIRAL GALAXIES

Spirals are characterized by circular symmetry, a bright nucleus surrounded by a thin outer disk, and a superimposed spiral structure. They are divided into two parallel classes: normal spirals and barred spirals. The normal spirals have arms that emanate from the nucleus, while barred spirals have a bright linear feature called a bar that straddles the nucleus, with the arms unwinding from the ends of the bar. The nucleus of a spiral galaxy is a sharp-peaked area of smooth texture, which can be quite small or, in some cases, can make up the bulk of the galaxy.

Both the arms and the disk of a spiral system are blue in colour, whereas its central areas are red like an elliptical galaxy. The normal spirals are designated S and the barred varieties SB. Each of these classes is subclassified into three types according to the size of the nucleus and the degree to which the spiral arms are coiled. The three types are denoted with the lowercase letters *a*, *b*, and *c*. There also exist galaxies that are intermediate between ellipticals

The Pinwheel Galaxy (M101), as seen in an optical image taken by the Hubble Space Telescope.

and spirals. Such systems have the disk shape characteristic of the latter but no spiral arms. These intermediate forms bear the designation S0.

S0 GALAXIES

These systems exhibit some of the properties of both the ellipticals and the spirals and seem to be a bridge between these two more common galaxy types. Hubble introduced the S0 class long after his original classification scheme had been universally adopted, largely because he noticed the dearth of highly flattened objects that otherwise had the properties of elliptical galaxies. Sandage's elaboration of the S0 class yielded the characteristics described here.

S0 galaxies have a bright nucleus that is surrounded by a smooth, featureless bulge and a faint outer envelope. They are thin; statistical studies of the ratio of the apparent axes (seen projected onto the sky) indicate that they have intrinsic ratios of minor to major axes in the range 0.1 to 0.3. Their structure does not generally follow the luminosity law of elliptical galaxies but has a form more like that for spiral galaxies. Some S0 systems have a hint of structure in the envelope, either faintly discernible armlike discontinuities or narrow absorption lanes produced by interstellar dust. Several S0 galaxies are otherwise peculiar, and it is difficult to classify them with certainty. They can be thought of as peculiar irregular galaxies (i.e., Irr II

Galaxy NGC 4753.

galaxies) or simply as some of the 1 or 2 percent of galaxies that do not fit easily into the Hubble scheme. Among these are such galaxies as NGC 4753, which has irregular dust lanes across its image, and NGC 128, which has a double, almost rectangular bulge around a central nucleus. Another type of peculiar S0 is found in NGC 2685. This nebula in the constellation Ursa Major has an apparently edge-on disk galaxy at its centre, with surrounding hoops of gas, dust, and stars arranged in a plane that is at right angles to the apparent plane of the central object.

Sb galaxy NGC 891 as seen edge-on in an optical image taken with the WIYN Telescope at the Kitt Peak National Observatory in Arizona, U.S. The dark band is made of interstellar dust.

SA GALAXIES

These normal spirals have narrow, tightly wound arms, which usually are visible because of the presence of interstellar dust and, in many cases, bright stars. Most of them have a large amorphous bulge in the centre, but there are some that violate this criterion, having a small nucleus around which is arranged an amorphous disk with superimposed faint arms. NGC 1302 is an example of the normal type of Sa galaxy, while NGC 4866 is representative of one with a small nucleus and arms consisting of thin dust lanes on a smooth disk.

SB GALAXIES

This intermediate type of spiral typically has a medium-sized nucleus. Its arms are more widely spread than those of the Sa variety and appear less smooth. They contain stars, star clouds, and interstellar gas and dust. Sb galaxies

ANDROMEDA GALAXY

The great spiral Andromeda Galaxy (M31) is the nearest external galaxy (except for the Magellanic Clouds, which are companions of the Milky Way Galaxy, in which Earth is located). The Andromeda Galaxy is one of the few visible to the unaided eye, appearing as a milky blur. It is located about 2,480,000 light-years from Earth; its diameter is approximately 200,000 light-years; and it shares various characteristics with the Milky Way system. It was mentioned as early as 965 CE, in the *Book of the Fixed Stars*, by the Islamic astronomer Al-Ṣūfī and rediscovered in 1612, shortly after the invention of the telescope, by the German astronomer Simon Marius, who said it resembled the light of a candle seen through a horn. For centuries astronomers regarded the Andromeda Galaxy as a component of the Milky Way Galaxy—i.e., as a so-called spiral nebula much like other glowing masses of gas within the local galactic system (hence the misnomer Andromeda Nebula). Only in the 1920s did the American astronomer Edwin Powell Hubble determine conclusively that the Andromeda was in fact a separate galaxy beyond the Milky Way.

The Andromeda Galaxy has a past involving

collisions with and accretion of other galaxies. Its peculiar close companion, M32, shows a structure that indicates that it was formerly a normal, more massive galaxy that lost much of its outer parts and possibly all of its globular clusters to M31 in a past encounter. Deep surveys of the outer parts of the Andromeda Galaxy have revealed huge coherent structures of star streams and clouds, with properties indicating that these include the outer remnants of smaller galaxies "eaten" by the giant central galaxy, as well as clouds of M31 stars ejected by the strong tidal forces of the collision.

show wide dispersions in details in terms of their shape. Hubble and Sandage observed, for example, that in certain Sb galaxies the arms emerge at the nucleus, which is often quite small. Other members of this subclass have arms that begin tangent to a bright, nearly circular ring, while still others reveal a small, bright spiral pattern inset into the nuclear bulge. In any of these cases, the spiral arms may be set at different pitch angles. (A pitch angle is defined as the angle between an arm and a circle centred on the nucleus and intersecting the arm.)

Hubble and Sandage noted further deviations from the standard shape established for Sb galaxies. A few systems exhibit a chaotic dust pattern superimposed upon the tightly wound spiral arms. Some have smooth, thick arms of low surface brightness, frequently bounded on their inner edges with dust lanes. Finally, there are those with a large, smooth nuclear bulge from which the arms emanate, owing outward tangent to the bulge and forming short arm segments. This is the most familiar type of Sb galaxy and is best exemplified by the giant Andromeda Galaxy.

Many of these variations in shape remain unexplained. Theoretical models of spiral galaxies based on a number of different premises can reproduce the basic Sb galaxy shape, but many of the deviations noted above are somewhat mysterious in origin and must await more detailed and realistic modeling of galactic dynamics.

SC GALAXIES

These galaxies characteristically have a very small nucleus and multiple spiral arms that are open, with relatively large pitch angles. The arms, moreover, are lumpy, containing as they do numerous irregularly distributed star clouds, stellar associations, star clusters, and gas clouds known as emission nebulae.

As in the case of Sb galaxies, there are several recognizable subtypes among the Sc systems. Sandage has cited six subdivisions: (1) galaxies, such as the Whirlpool Galaxy (M51), that have thin branched arms that wind outward from a tiny nucleus, usually extending out about 180° before branching into multiple segments, (2) systems with multiple arms that start tangent to a bright ring centred on the nucleus, (3) those with arms that are poorly defined and that span the entire image of the galaxy, (4) those with a spiral pattern that cannot easily be traced and that are multiple and punctuated with chaotic dust lanes, (5) those with thick, loose arms that are not well defined—e.g., the nearby galaxy M33 (the Triangulum Nebula)—and (6) transition types, which are almost so lacking in order that they could be considered irregular galaxies.

Some classification schemes, such as that of the French-born American astronomer Gerard de Vaucouleurs, give the last of the above-cited subtypes a class of its own, type Sd. It also has been found that some of the variations noted here for Sc galaxies are related to total luminosity. Galaxies of the fifth subtype, in particular, tend to be intrinsically faint, while those of the first subtype are among the most luminous spirals known.

SB GALAXIES

The luminosities, dimensions, spectra, and distributions of barred spirals tend to be indistinguishable from those of normal spirals. Subclasses of SB systems exist in parallel sequence to those of the latter.

Barred spiral galaxy NGC 1300.

There are SB0 galaxies that feature a large nuclear bulge surrounded by a disk-like envelope across which runs a luminous featureless bar. Some SB0 systems have short bars, while others have bars that extend across the entire visible image. Occasionally there is a ringlike feature external to the bar. SBa galaxies have bright, fairly large nuclear bulges and tightly wound, smooth spiral arms that emerge from the ends of the bar or from a circular ring external to the bar. SBb systems have a smooth bar as well as relatively smooth and continuous arms. In some galaxies of this type, the arms start at or near the ends of the bar, with conspicuous dust lanes along the inside of the bar that can be traced right up to the nucleus. Others have arms that start tangent to a ring external to the bar. In SBc galaxies, both the arms and the bar are highly resolved into star clouds and stellar associations. The arms are open in form and can start either at the ends of the bar or tangent to a ring.

IRREGULAR GALAXIES

Most representatives of this class consist of grainy, highly irregular assemblages of luminous areas. They have neither noticeable symmetry nor an obvious central nucleus, and they are generally bluer in colour than are the arms and disks of spiral galaxies. An extremely small number of them, however, are red and have a smooth, though non-symmetrical, shape.

Hubble recognized these two types of irregular galaxies, Irr I and Irr II. The Irr I type is the most common of the irregular systems, and it seems to fall naturally on an extension of the spiral classes, beyond Sc, into galaxies with no discernible spiral structure. They are blue, are highly resolved, and have little or no nucleus. The Irr II systems are red, rare objects. They include various kinds of chaotic galaxies for which there apparently are many different explanations, including most commonly the results of galaxy-galaxy interactions, both tidal distortions and

The Cigar Galaxy, M82.

cannibalism; therefore, this category is no longer seen as a useful way to classify galaxies.

Some irregular galaxies, like spirals, are barred. They have a nearly central bar structure dominating an otherwise chaotic arrangement of material. The Large Magellanic Cloud is a well-known example.

OTHER TYPES OF GALAXIES

Other classification schemes similar to Hubble's follow his pattern but subdivide the galaxies differently. A notable example of one such system is that of de Vaucouleurs. This scheme, which has evolved considerably since its inception in 1959, includes a large number of codes for indicating different kinds of morphological characteristics visible in the images of galaxies. The major Hubble galaxy classes form the framework of de Vaucouleurs's scheme, and its subdivision includes different families, varieties, and stages. The de Vaucouleurs system is so detailed that it is more of a descriptive code for galaxies than a commonly used classification scheme.

Galaxies with unusual properties often have shorthand names that refer to their characteristic properties. Common examples are:

D: Galaxies with abnormally large, distended shapes, always found in the central areas of galaxy clusters and hypothesized to consist of merged galaxies.

S: Seyfert galaxies, originally recognized by the American astronomer Carl K. Seyfert from optical spectra. These objects have very bright nuclei with strong emission lines of hydrogen and other common elements, showing velocities of hundreds or thousands of kilometres per second. Most are radio sources.

N: Galaxies with small, very bright nuclei and strong radio emission. These are probably similar to Seyfert galaxies but more distant.

Q: Quasars, or QSOs, small, extremely luminous objects, many of which are strong radio sources. Quasars apparently are related to Seyfert and N galaxies but have such bright nuclei that the underlying galaxy can be detected only with great difficulty.

There are also different schemes used for extremely distant galaxies, which we see in their youth. When a very distant galaxy is examined with a very large telescope, we see its structure as it was when the light was emitted billions of years ago. In such cases, the distinctive Hubble types are not so obvious. Apparently, galaxies are much less well organized in their early years, and these very distant objects tend to be highly irregular and asymmetrical. Although special classification schemes are sometimes used for special purposes, the general scheme of Hubble in its updated form is the one most commonly used.

CHAPTER 4

GALAXIES OTHER THAN OUR OWN

It is difficult for an observer to imagine that there are an estimated 2 trillion galaxies in the universe. We look up at the night sky and all the observable stars belong to our own Milky Way. However, beyond the Milky Way stretches the vast universe filled with galaxies.

The range in intrinsic size for the external galaxies, or galaxies beyond the Milky Way Galaxy, extends from the smallest systems, such as the extreme dwarf galaxies found near the Milky Way that are only 100 light years across, to giant radio galaxies, the extent of which (including their radio-bright lobes) is more than 3,000,000 light-years. Normal large spiral galaxies, such as the Andromeda Galaxy, have diameters of 100,000 to 500,000 light-years.

The total masses of galaxies are not well known, largely because of the uncertain nature of the hypothesized invisible dark halos that surround many, or possibly all, galaxies. The total mass of material within the radius out to which the stars or gas of a galaxy can be detected is known for many hundreds of systems. The range is from about 100,000 to roughly 1,000,000,000,000 times the Sun's mass. The mass of a typical large spiral is about 500,000,000,000 Suns.

In the late 20th century it became clear that most of the mass in galaxies is not in the form of stars or other visible matter. By measuring the speed with which stars in spiral and elliptical galaxies orbit the centre of the galaxy, one can measure the mass inside that orbit. Most galaxies have more mass than can be accounted for by their stars. Therefore, there is some unidentified "dark matter" that dominates the dynamics of most galaxies. The dark matter seems to be distributed more broadly than the stars in galaxies. Extensive efforts to identify this dark matter have not yet been satisfactory, though the detection of large numbers of very faint stars, including brown dwarfs, was in some sense a byproduct of these searches, as was the discovery of the mass of neutrinos. It is somewhat frustrating for astronomers to know that the majority of the mass in galaxies (and in the universe) is of an unknown nature.

LUMINOSITY OF EXTERNAL GALAXIES

The external galaxies show an extremely large range in their total luminosities. The intrinsically faintest are the extreme dwarf elliptical galaxies, such as the Ursa Minor dwarf, which has a luminosity of approximately 100,000

Suns. The most luminous galaxies are those that contain quasars at their centres. These remarkably bright superactive nuclei can be as luminous as 2,000,000,000,000 Suns. The underlying galaxies are often as much as 100 times fainter than their nuclei. Normal large spiral galaxies have a luminosity of a few hundred billion Suns.

AGE

Even though different galaxies have had quite different histories, measurements tend to suggest that most, if not all, galaxies have very nearly the same age. The age of the Milky Way Galaxy, which is measured by determining the ages of the oldest stars found within it, is approximately 13 billion years. Nearby galaxies, even those such as the Large and Small Magellanic Clouds that contain a multitude of very young stars, also have at least a few very old stars of approximately that same age. When more distant galaxies are examined, their spectra and colours closely resemble those of the nearby galaxies, and it is inferred that they too must contain a population of similarly very old stars. Extremely distant galaxies, on the other hand, look younger, but that is because the "look-back" time for them is a significant fraction of their age; the light received from such galaxies was emitted when they were appreciably younger.

It seems likely that all the galaxies began to form about the same time, when the universe had cooled down enough for matter to condense, and they all thus started forming stars during nearly the same epoch. Their large differences are a matter not of age but rather of how they proceeded to regulate the processing of their materials (gas and dust) into stars. Some ellipticals formed almost all their stars during the first few billion years, while others may have had a more complicated history, including various periods of active star formation related to the merging together of smaller galaxies. In a merging event the gas can be compressed, which enhances the conditions necessary for new bursts of star formation. The spirals and the irregulars, on the other hand, have been using up their materials more gradually.

COMPOSITION OF EXTERNAL GALAXIES

The abundances of the chemical elements in stars and galaxies are remarkably uniform. The ratios of the amounts of the different elements that astronomers observe for the Sun are a reasonably good approximation for those of other stars in the Milky Way Galaxy and also for stars in other galaxies. The main difference found is in the relative amount of the primordial gases, hydrogen and helium. The heavier elements are formed by stellar evolutionary processes, and they are relatively more abundant in areas where extensive star formation has been taking place. Thus, in such small elliptical galaxies as the Draco system, where almost all the stars were formed at the beginning of its lifetime, the component stars are nearly pure hydrogen and helium. In such large galaxies as the Andromeda Galaxy there are areas where star formation has been active for a long time (right up to the present, in fact), and there investigators find that the heavier elements are more abundant. In some external galaxies as well as in some parts of the Milky Way Galaxy system, heavy elements are even more abundant than in the Sun but rarely by more than a factor of two or so. Even in such cases, hydrogen and helium make up most of the constituent materials, accounting for at least 90 percent of the mass.

The spiral arms of some galaxies are the most notable part of their structure. However, there are other no less important pieces of a galaxy from a halo of old stars to its interstellar gas.

Most and perhaps all galaxies have a spheroidal component of old stars. In the ellipticals this component constitutes all or most of any given system. In the spirals it represents about half the constituent stars (this fraction varies greatly according to galaxy type).

In the irregulars the spheroidal component is very inconspicuous or, possibly in some cases, entirely absent. The structure of the spheroidal component of all galaxies is similar, as if the spirals and irregulars possess a skeleton of old stars arranged in a structure that resembles an elliptical.

One of the open questions about the structure of these objects is why they have as much flattening as some of them do. In most cases, the measured rotation rate is inadequate to explain the flattening on the basis of a model of an oblate spheroid that rotates around its short axis. Some elliptical galaxies are instead prolate spheroids that rotate around their long axis.

Except for such early-type galaxies as S0, SB0, Sa, and SBa systems, spirals and irregulars have a flat component of stars that emits most of their brightness. The disk component has a thickness that is approximately one-fifth its diameter (this varies, depending on the type of stars being considered). The stars show a radial distribution that obeys an exponential decrease outward.

The structure of the arms of spiral galaxies depends on the galaxy type, and there is also a great deal of variability within each type. Generally, the early Hubble types have smooth, indistinct spiral arms with small pitch angles. The later types have more-open arms (larger pitch angles). Within a given type there can be found galaxies that have extensive arms (extending around the centre for two or more complete rotations) and those that have a chaotic arm structure made up of many short fragments that extend only 20° or 30° around the centre.

If one were to look at galaxies at wavelengths that show only neutral hydrogen gas, they would look rather different from their optical appearance. Normally the gas, as detected at radio wavelengths for neutral hydrogen atoms, is more widely spread out, with the size of the gas component often extending to twice the size of the optically visible image. Also, in some galaxies a hole exists in the centre of the system where almost no neutral hydrogen occurs. There is, however, enough molecular hydrogen to make up for the lack of atomic hydrogen. Molecular hydrogen is difficult to detect, but it is accompanied by other molecules, such as carbon monoxide, which can be observed at radio wavelengths.

GALAXY CLUSTERS

Galaxies tend to cluster together, sometimes in small groups and sometimes in enormous complexes. Most galaxies have companions, either a few nearby objects or a large-scale cluster; isolated galaxies, in other words, are quite rare.

There are several different classification schemes for galaxy clusters, but the simplest is the most useful. This scheme divides clusters into three classes: groups, irregulars, and sphericals.

The groups class is composed of small compact groups of 10 to 50 galaxies of mixed types, spanning roughly

Hickson Compact Group 87, which contains four galaxies, as seen in an optical image taken by the Hubble Space Telescope.

five million light-years. An example of such an entity is the Local Group, which includes the Milky Way Galaxy, the Magellanic Clouds, the Andromeda Galaxy, and about 50 other systems, mostly of the dwarf variety.

Irregular clusters are large loosely structured assemblages of mixed galaxy types (mostly spirals and ellipticals), totaling perhaps 1,000 or more systems and extending out 10,000,000 to 50,000,000 light-years. The Virgo and Hercules clusters are representative of this class.

Spherical clusters are dense and consist almost exclusively of elliptical and S0 galaxies. They are enormous, having a linear diameter of up to 50,000,000 light-years. Spherical clusters may contain as many as 10,000 galaxies, which are concentrated toward the cluster centre.

Markarians Chain galaxies that form part of the Virgo Cluster.

DISTRIBUTION OF CLUSTERS

Clusters of galaxies are found all over the sky. They are difficult to detect along the Milky Way, where high concentrations of the Milky Way Galaxy's dust and gas obscure virtually everything at optical wavelengths. However, even there clusters can be found in a few galactic "windows," random holes in the dust that permit optical observations.

The clusters are not evenly spaced in the sky; instead, they are arranged in a way that suggests a certain amount

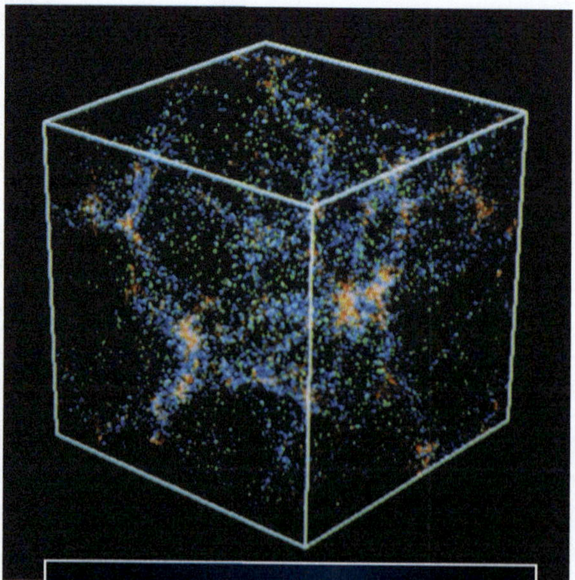

Computer simulation of a portion of the universe, modeling the distribution of 10,000 galaxies.

of organization. Clusters are frequently associated with other clusters, forming giant superclusters. These superclusters typically consist of 3 to 10 clusters and span as many as 200 million light-years. There also are immense areas between clusters that are fairly empty, forming voids.

Large-scale surveys made in the 1980s of the radial velocities of galaxies revealed an even-larger kind of structure. It was discovered that galaxies and galaxy clusters tend to fall in position along large planes and curves, almost like giant walls, with relatively empty spaces between them. A related large-scale structure was found to exist where there occur departures from the velocity-distance relation in certain directions, indicating that the otherwise uniform expansion is being perturbed by large concentrations of mass. One of these, discovered in 1988, has been dubbed "the Great Attractor."

HOW CLUSTER MEMBERS INTERACT

Galaxies in clusters exist in a part of the universe that is much denser than average, and the result is that they have several unusual features. In the inner parts of dense clusters there are very few, if any, normal spiral galaxies. This condition is probably the result of fairly frequent collisions between the closely packed galaxies, as such violent interactions tend to sweep out the interstellar gas, leaving behind only the spherical component and a gasless disk. What remains is in effect an S0 galaxy.

A second and related effect of galaxy interactions is the presence of gas-poor spiral systems at the centres of large irregular clusters. A significant number of the members of such clusters have anomalously small amounts of neutral hydrogen, and their gas components are smaller on average than those for more isolated galaxies. This is thought to be the result of frequent distant encounters between such galaxies involving the disruption of their outer parts.

A third effect of the dense cluster environment is the presence in some clusters—usually rather small dense clusters—of an unusual type of galaxy called a cD galaxy. These objects are somewhat similar in structure to S0 galaxies, but they are considerably larger, having envelopes that extend out to radii as large as one million light-years. Many of them have multiple nuclei, and most are strong

The Antennae galaxies colliding.

sources of radio waves. The most likely explanation for cD galaxies is that they are massive central galactic systems that have captured smaller cluster members because of their dominating gravitational fields and have absorbed the other galaxies into their own structures. Astronomers sometimes refer to this process as galactic cannibalism. In this sense, the outer extended disks of cD systems, as well as their multiple nuclei, represent the remains of past partly digested "meals."

One more effect that can be traced to the cluster environment is the presence of strong radio and X-ray sources, which tend to occur in or near the centres of clusters of galaxies.

RADIO GALAXIES

Some of the strongest radio sources in the sky are galaxies. Most of them have a peculiar morphology that is related to the cause of their radio radiation. Some are relatively isolated galaxies, but most galaxies that emit unusually large amounts of radio energy are found in large clusters.

The basic characteristics of radio galaxies and the variations that exist among them can be made clear with two examples. The first is Centaurus A, a giant radio structure surrounding a bright, peculiar galaxy of remarkable morphology designated NGC 5128. It exemplifies a type of radio galaxy that consists of an optical galaxy located at the centre of an immensely larger two-lobed radio source.

In the particular case of Centaurus A, the extent of the radio structure is so great that it is almost 100 times the size of the central galaxy, which is itself a giant galaxy. This radio structure includes, besides the pair of far-flung radio lobes, two other sets of radio sources: one that is approximately the size of the optical galaxy and that resembles the outer structure in shape, and a second that

The giant elliptical galaxy NGC 5128, show here in visible light, hosts the radio source known as Centaurus A.

is an intense small source at the galaxy's nucleus.

Optically, NGC 5128 appears as a giant elliptical galaxy with two notable characteristics: an unusual disk of dust and gas surrounding it and thin jets of interstellar gas and young stars radiating outward. The most plausible explanation for this whole array is that a series of energetic events in the nucleus of the galaxy expelled hot ionized gas from the centre at relativistic velocities (i.e., those at nearly the speed of light) in two opposite directions. These clouds of relativistic particles generate synchrotron radiation, which is detected at radio (and X-ray) wavelengths. In this model the very large structure is associated with an old event, while the inner lobes are the result of more-recent ejections. The centre is still active, as evidenced by the presence of the nuclear radio source.

The other notable example of a radio galaxy is Virgo A, a powerful radio source that corresponds to a bright elliptical galaxy in the Virgo cluster, designated as M87. In this type of radio galaxy, most of the radio radiation is emitted from an appreciably smaller area than in the case of Centaurus A. This area coincides in size with the optically visible object. Virgo A is not particularly unusual except for one peculiarity: it has a bright jet of gaseous material that appears to emanate from the nucleus of the galaxy, extending out approximately halfway to its faint outer parts. This gaseous jet can be detected at optical, radio, and other (e.g., X-ray) wavelengths; its spectrum suggests strongly that it shines by means of the synchrotron mechanism.

About the only condition that can account for the immense amounts of energy emitted by radio galaxies is the capture of material (interstellar gas and stars) by a supermassive object at their centre. Such an object would resemble the one thought to be in the nucleus of the Milky Way Galaxy but would be far more massive. In short, the most probable type of supermassive object for explaining the details of strong radio sources would be a black hole. Large amounts of energy can be released when material is captured by a black hole. An extremely hot high-density accretion disk is first formed around the supermassive object from the material, and then some of the material seems to be ejected explosively from the area, giving rise to

VIRGO A

Virgo A is a giant elliptical galaxy in the constellation Virgo whose nucleus provides the strongest observational evidence for the existence of a black hole. Virgo A is the most powerful known source of radio energy among the thousands of galactic systems comprising the so-called Virgo Cluster. It is also a powerful X-ray source, which suggests the presence of very hot gas in the galaxy. A luminous gaseous jet projects outward from the galactic nucleus. Both the jet and the nucleus emit synchrotron radiation, a form of nonthermal radiation released by charged particles that are accelerated in magnetic fields and travel at speeds near that of light. Virgo A lies about 50 million light-years from the Earth.

In 1994 the Hubble Space Telescope obtained images of Virgo A that showed a disk of hot, ionized gas about 500 light-years in diameter at a distance of about 60 light-years from the galaxy's centre. The disk's gases are revolving about the nucleus at a speed of about 550 km per second, or about 1.9 million km (1.2 million miles) per hour, a velocity so great that only the gravitational pull of an object with a mass two to three billion times that of the Sun would be capable of holding the disk together. This supermassive object could occupy a region as small as the galactic nucleus only if it were a black hole. Gravitational energy released by gas spiraling down into the black hole produces a beam of electrons accelerated almost to the speed of light; the bright gaseous jet that emanates from Virgo A is thought to be radiation from this beam of electrons.

the various radio jets and lobes observed.

Another kind of event that can result in an explosive eruption around a nuclear black hole involves cases of merging galaxies in which the nuclei of the galaxies "collide." Because many, if not most, galaxy nuclei contain a black hole, such a collision can generate an immense amount of energy as the black holes merge.

X-RAY GALAXIES

Synchrotron radiation is characteristically emitted at virtually all wavelengths at almost the same intensity. A synchrotron source therefore ought to be detectable at optical and radio wavelengths, as well as at others (e.g., infrared, ultraviolet, X-ray, and gamma-ray wavelengths). For radio galaxies this does seem to be the case, at least in circumstances where the radiation is not screened by absorbing material in the source or in intervening space.

X-rays are absorbed by Earth's atmosphere. Consequently, X-ray galaxies could not be detected until it became possible to place telescopes above the atmosphere, first with balloons and sounding rockets and later with orbiting observatories specially designed for X-ray studies. For example, the Einstein Observatory, which was in operation during the early 1980s, made a fairly complete search for X-ray sources across the sky and studied several of them in detail. Beginning in 1999, the Chandra X-ray Observatory and other orbiting X-ray observatories detected huge numbers of emitters. Many of the sources turned out to be distant galaxies and quasars, while others were relatively nearby objects, including neutron stars (extremely dense stars composed almost exclusively of neutrons) in the Milky Way Galaxy.

A substantial number of the X-ray galaxies so far detected are also well-known radio galaxies. Some X-ray sources, such as certain radio sources, are much too large to be individual galaxies but rather consist of a whole cluster of galaxies.

RADIO AND X-RAY SOURCES

Some clusters of galaxies contain a widespread intergalactic cloud of hot gas that can be detected as a diffuse radio source or as a large-scale source of X-rays. The gaseous cloud has a low density but a very high temperature, having been heated by the motion of the cluster's galaxies through it and by the emission of high-energy particles from active galaxies within it.

The form of certain radio galaxies in clusters points rather strongly to the presence of intergalactic gas. These are the "head-tail" galaxies, systems that have a bright source accompanied by a tail or tails that appear swept back by their interaction with the cooler more stationary intergalactic gas. These tails are radio lobes of ejected gas whose shape has been distorted by collisions with the cluster medium.

QUASARS

An apparently new kind of radio source was discovered in the early 1960s when radio astronomers identified a very small but powerful radio object designated 3C 48 with a stellar optical image. When they obtained the spectrum of the optical object, they found unexpected and at first unexplainable emission lines superimposed on a flat continuum. This object remained a mystery until another similar but optically brighter object, 3C 273, was examined in 1963. Investigators noticed that 3C 273 had a normal spectrum with the same emission lines as observed in radio galaxies, though greatly redshifted (i.e., the spectral lines are displaced to longer wavelengths), as by the Doppler effect. If the redshift were to be ascribed to velocity, however, it would imply an immense velocity of recession. In the case of 3C 48, the redshift had been so large as to shift familiar lines so far that they were not recognized. Many more such objects were found, and they came to be known as quasi-stellar radio sources, abbreviated as quasars.

Although the first 20 years of quasar studies were noted more for controversy and mystery than for progress in understanding, subsequent years finally saw a solution

Six quasar host galaxies, as observed by the Hubble Space Telescope. Shown are apparently normal, solitary galaxies *(left)*, colliding galaxies *(centre)*, and merging galaxies *(right)*.

to the questions raised by these strange objects. It is now clear that quasars are extreme examples of energetic galaxy nuclei. The amount of radiation emitted by such a nucleus overwhelms the light from the rest of the galaxy, so only very special observational techniques can reveal the galaxy's existence.

A quasar has many remarkable properties. Although it is extremely small (only the size of the solar system), it emits up to 100 times as much radiation as an entire galaxy. It is a complex mixture of very hot gas, cooler gas and dust, and particles that emit synchrotron radiation. Its brightness often varies over short periods—days or even hours. The galaxy underlying the brilliant image of a quasar may be fairly normal in some of its properties except for the superficial large-scale effects of the quasar at its centre. Quasars apparently are powered by the same mechanism attributed to radio galaxies. They demonstrate in an extreme way what a supermassive object at the centre of a galaxy can do.

With the gradual recognition of the causes of the quasar phenomenon has come an equally gradual realization that they are simply extreme examples of a process that can be observed in more familiar objects. The black holes that are thought to inhabit the cores of the quasar galaxies are similar to, though more explosive than, those that appear to occur in certain unusual nearer galaxies known as Seyfert galaxies. The radio galaxies fall in between. The reason for the differences in the level of activity is apparently related to the source of the gas and stars that are falling into the centres of such objects, providing the black holes with fuel.

In the case of quasars, evidence suggests that an encounter with another galaxy, which causes the latter to be tidally destroyed and its matter to fall into the centre of the more massive quasar galaxy, may be the cause of its activity. As the material approaches the black hole, it is greatly accelerated, and some of it is expelled by the prevailing high temperatures and drastically rapid motions. This process probably also explains the impressive but lower-level activity in the nuclei of radio and Seyfert galaxies. The captured mass may be of lesser amount—i.e., either a smaller galaxy or a portion of the host galaxy itself. Quasars are more common in that part of the universe observed to have redshifts of about 2, meaning that they were more common about 10 or so billion years ago than they are now, which is at least partly a result of the higher density of galaxies at that time.

GAMMA-RAY BURSTERS

In the 1970s a new type of object was identified as using orbiting gamma-ray detectors. These "gamma-ray bursters" are identified by extremely energetic bursts of gamma radiation that last only seconds. In some cases the bursters are clearly identified with very distant galaxies, implying immense energies in the bursts. In one case, gravitational waves have been observed from a gamma-ray burst, identifying the source as two neutron stars merging in a galaxy 130 million light-years away. Many gamma-ray bursts were detected by Swift, a U.S. satellite observatory that swings into the proper orientation to catch the first few seconds of the bursts.

COMA CLUSTER

The Coma cluster is the nearest rich cluster of galaxies; it contains thousands of systems. The Coma cluster lies about 33 million light-years away, about seven times farther than the Virgo cluster, in the direction of the constellation Coma Berenices. The main body of the Coma cluster has a diameter of about 2.5 x 10^7 light-years, but enhancements above the background can be traced out to a supercluster of a diameter of about 2 x 10^8 light-years. Ellipticals or S0s constitute 85 percent of the bright galaxies in the Coma cluster; the two brightest ellipticals in Coma are located near the centre of the system and are individually more than 10 times as luminous as the Andromeda Galaxy. These galaxies have a swarm of smaller companions orbiting them and may have grown to their bloated sizes by a process of "galactic cannibalism" like that hypothesized to explain the supergiant elliptical cD systems.

The spatial distribution of galaxies in rich clusters such as the Coma cluster closely resembles what one would expect theoretically for a bound set of bodies moving in the collective gravitational field of the system. Yet, if one measures the dispersion of random velocities of the Coma galaxies about the mean, one finds that it amounts to almost 900 km per second (500 miles per second). For a galaxy possessing this random velocity along a typical line of sight to be gravitationally bound within the known dimensions of the cluster requires Coma to have a total mass of about 5 x 10^{15} solar masses. The total luminosity of the Coma cluster is measured to be about 3 x 10^{13} solar luminosities; therefore, the mass-to-light ratio in solar units required to explain Coma as a bound system exceeds by an order of magnitude what can be reasonably ascribed to the known stellar populations. A similar situation exists for every rich cluster that has been examined in detail. When Swiss astronomer Fritz Zwicky discovered this discrepancy in 1933, he inferred that much of the Coma cluster was made of nonluminous matter. The existence of nonluminous matter, or "dark matter," was later confirmed in the 1970s by American astronomers Vera Rubin and W. Kent Ford.

CYGNUS A

Cygnus A is the most powerful cosmic source of radio waves known, lying in the northern constellation

Cygnus about 750,000,000 light-years from Earth. It has the appearance of a double galaxy. For a time it was thought to be two galaxies in collision, but the energy output is too large to be accounted for in that way. Radio energy is emitted from Cygnus A at an estimated 10^{45} ergs per second, more than 10^{11} times the rate at which energy of all kinds is emitted by the Sun. The source of the energy of Cygnus A is a supermassive black hole 2.5 billion times the mass of the Sun.

GREAT ATTRACTOR

The Great Attractor is a proposed concentration of mass that influences the movement of many galaxies, including the Milky Way. In 1986 a group of astronomers observing the motions of the Milky Way and neighbouring galaxies noted that the galaxies were moving toward the Hydra-Centaurus superclusters in the southern sky with velocities significantly different from those predicted by the expansion of the universe in accordance with the Hubble law. One possible explanation for this perturbation in the Hubble flow is the existence of the so-called Great Attractor—a region or structure of huge mass (equivalent to tens of thousands of galaxies) exerting a gravitational pull on the surrounding galaxies. It is estimated that the Great Attractor would have a diameter of about 300 million light-years and that its centre would lie about 147 million light-years away from Earth.

MAGELLANIC CLOUDS

The Magellanic Clouds are two satellite galaxies of the Milky Way Galaxy, the vast star system of which Earth is a minor component. These companion galaxies were named for the Portuguese navigator Ferdinand Magellan, whose crew discovered them during the first voyage around the world (1519–22).

The Magellanic Clouds are irregular galaxies that share a gaseous envelope and lie about 22° apart in the sky near the south celestial pole. One of them, the Large Magellanic Cloud (LMC), is a luminous patch about 5° in diameter, and the other, the Small Magellanic Cloud (SMC), measures less than 2° across. The Magellanic Clouds are visible to the unaided eye in the Southern Hemisphere, but they cannot be observed from the northern latitudes. The LMC is about 163,000 light-years from Earth, and the SMC lies 202,000 light-years away. The LMC and SMC are 14,000 and 7,000 light-years in diameter, respectively, and are smaller than the Milky Way Galaxy, which is about 140,000 light-years across.

The Magellanic Clouds were formed at about the same time as the Milky Way Galaxy, approximately 13 billion years ago. They are presently captured in orbits around the Galaxy and have experienced several tidal encounters with each other and with the Galaxy. They contain numerous young stars and star clusters, as well as some much older stars. The Magellanic Clouds serve as excellent laboratories for the study of very active stellar formation and evolution. With the Hubble Space Telescope it is possible for astronomers to study the kinds of stars, star clusters, and nebulae that previously could be observed in great detail only in the Galaxy.

M81 GROUP

The M81 group of more than 40 galaxies is found at a distance of 12 million light-years from Earth, one of the nearest galaxy groups to the Local Group (the group of galaxies that includes the Milky Way Galaxy). The dominant galaxy in the M81 group is the spiral galaxy M81. Much like the Andromeda and Milky Way galaxies, M81 is of Hubble type Sb and luminosity class II.

There are two subgroups in the M81 group: one group is associated with M81 and another is associated with the spiral galaxy NGC 2403. These two subgroups are moving toward each other. The total mass of the M81 group has been determined from the motion of galaxies within it to be 1012 solar masses. M81 has a mass of 6.7 x 1011 solar masses.

The M81 group also has a few galaxies with classifications similar to those of galaxies in the Local Group, and it was noticed by some astronomers that the linear sizes of the largest H II regions (which are illuminated by many OB stars) in these galaxies had about the same intrinsic sizes as their counterparts in the Local Group. This led American astronomer Allan Sandage and the German chemist and physicist Gustav Tammann to the (controversial) technique of using the sizes of H II regions as a distance indicator, because a measurement of their angular sizes, coupled with knowledge of their linear sizes, allows an inference of distance.

MAFFEI 1 AND 2

The two galaxies Maffei 1 and 2 are relatively close to the Milky Way Galaxy but were unobserved until the late 1960s, when the Italian astronomer Paolo Maffei detected them by their infrared radiation. Studies in the United States established that the objects are galaxies. Lying near the border between the constellations Perseus and Cassiopeia, they are close to the plane of the Milky Way, where obscuring dust clouds in interstellar space prevent nearly all visible light emitted by external galaxies from reaching Earth.

Maffei 1 is a large elliptical galaxy. It was once thought to belong to the Local Group of galaxies, of which the

Galaxy is a member, but it is now known to be about 9 million light-years away. Maffei 2 has a spiral structure and 10 million light-years distant.

VIRGO A

Virgo A (catalog numbers M87, and NGC 4486) is a giant elliptical galaxy in the constellation Virgo whose nucleus provides the strongest observational evidence for the existence of a black hole. Virgo A is the most powerful known source of radio energy among the thousands of galactic systems comprising the so-called Virgo cluster. It is also a powerful X-ray source, which suggests the presence of very hot gas in the galaxy. A luminous gaseous jet projects outward from the galactic nucleus. Both the jet and the nucleus emit synchrotron radiation, a form of nonthermal radiation released by charged particles that are accelerated in magnetic fields and travel at speeds near that of light. Virgo A lies about 50 million light-years from the Earth.

In 1994 the Hubble Space Telescope obtained images of Virgo A that showed a disk of hot, ionized gas about 500 light-years in diameter at a distance of about 60 light-years from the galaxy's centre. The disk's gases are revolving about the nucleus at a speed of about 550 km (341 miles) per second, or about 1.9 million km (1.2 million miles) per hour, a velocity so great that only the gravitational pull of an object with a mass six billion times that of the Sun would be capable of holding the disk together. This supermassive object could occupy a region as small as the galactic nucleus only if it were a black hole. Gravitational energy released by gas spiraling down into the black hole produces a beam of electrons accelerated almost to the speed of light; the bright gaseous jet that emanates from Virgo A is thought to be radiation from this beam of electrons.

VIRGO CLUSTER

The Virgo cluster is the closest large cluster of galaxies; it is located at a distance of about 5×10^7 light-years in the direction of the constellation Virgo. More than 2,000 galaxies reside in the Virgo cluster, scattered in various subclusters whose largest concentration (near the famous system M87 [Virgo A]) is about 5×10^6 light-years in diameter. Of the galaxies in the Virgo cluster, 58 percent are spirals, 27 percent are ellipticals, and the rest are irregulars. Although spirals are more numerous, the four brightest galaxies are giant ellipticals, among them Virgo A. Calibration of the absolute brightnesses of these giant ellipticals allows a leap to the measurement of distant regular clusters.

CONCLUSION

It is almost impossible to understand just how vast the universe is. One way we can bring it to scale, however, is by studying galaxies. To think that there can be trillions of stars within a single galaxy and that it is estimated that the universe contains over a trillion galaxies, we can begin to understand just how small we are.

From galaxies, we can also treat the possibility of extraterrestrial life as a probability. A significant percentage of the stars in the universe have planets that orbit them. Though many of those planets are not suitable for life, some are. They orbit within what's called the "Goldilocks Zone," just the right distance from their star for the planet to be of a temperature where life can thrive. Planets that are suited for life may be rare. However, from the sheer number of stars in our universe, simple statistics tells us that extraterrestrial life, in all likelihood, exists.

We are in a golden age of the study of galaxies. Each year brings new technologies that help scientists peer into the depths of space, and each day, scientists make new discoveries. With the countless galaxies that exist, there quite literally is a universe of exploration before us.

GLOSSARY

big bang The cosmic explosion that marked the beginning of the universe according to the big-bang theory.

binary stars A pair of stars in orbit around a common centre of gravity.

black hole An area in space with an intense gravitational field whose escape velocity exceeds the speed of light.

brown dwarf A celestial object that is much smaller than a normal star and has insufficient mass to sustain nuclear fusion but that is hot enough to radiate energy especially at infrared wavelengths.

dark matter Nonluminous matter not yet directly detected by astronomers that is hypothesized to exist to account for various observed gravitational effects.

density The mass of a unit volume of a material substance.

dwarf star A low-luminosity star.

element Any of the fundamental substances that consist of atoms of only one kind and that singly or in combination constitute all matter.

elliptical Of, relating to, or shaped like an ellipse.

galactic Of or relating to a galaxy.

globular cluster Any of various approximately spherical clusters of gravitationally associated stars that typically populate galactic halos.

interstellar Located, taking place, or traveling among the stars especially of the Milky Way galaxy.

Kelvin The base unit of temperature in the International System of Units that is equal to 1/273.16 of the Kelvin scale temperature of the triple point of water.

kinematics The study of motion.

light-year The distance traveled by light in one year and roughly 9,460,000,000,000 km [5,880,000,000,000 miles].

luminosity The relative quantity of radiation emitted by a celestial source.

magnetic field The portion of space near a magnetic body or a current-carrying body in which the magnetic forces due to the body or current can be detected.

mass The property of a body that is a measure of its inertia and that is commonly taken as a measure of the amount of material it contains and causes it to have weight in a gravitational field.

morphology A study of structure or form.

nebula A mass of interstellar gas and dust.

neutron star Any of a class of extremely dense, compact stars thought to be composed primarily of neutrons.

nova A star that brightens temporarily while ejecting a shell explosively.

nucleus The small brighter and denser portion of a galaxy.

primordial Existing in or persisting from the beginning (as of a solar system or universe).

quasar The abbreviation for quasi-stellar radio source, which emits up to 100 times as much radiation as an entire galaxy.

radiation Energy radiated in the form of waves or particles.

radio galaxy A galaxy that is a powerful source of radio waves.

radio telescope A radio receiver-antenna combination used for observation in radio astronomy.

Schwarzschild radius The radius of the spherical boundary within which a given mass (as of a star) must collapse to become a black hole.

spectrum Any of various continua that resemble a color spectrum in consisting of an ordered arrangement by a particular characteristic (such as frequency or energy).

spheroid A figure resembling a sphere.

supernova The explosion of a star in which the star may reach a maximum intrinsic luminosity one billion times that of the Sun.

synchrotron An apparatus for imparting very high speeds to charged particles by means of a combination of a high-frequency electric field and a low-frequency magnetic field.

tidal force The effect of the stretching of a body toward the centre of mass of another body due to the gradient in strength of the gravitational field.

wavelength The distance from one wave of energy to another as it is traveling from one point to another point.

THE MILKY WAY

Leila Belkora, *Minding the Heavens: The Story of Our Discovery of the Milky Way* (2003), is an interesting mix of history, biography, and science that describes how astronomers gradually uncovered the nature of the Milky Way. Linda S. Sparke and John S. Gallagher, *Galaxies in the Universe* (2000), gives a good basic introduction to galactic dynamics. Debra M. Elmegreen, *Galaxies and Galactic Structure* (1998), is an elementary text with an excellent chapter on galactic structure and kinematics. Dimitri Mihalas and James Binney, *Galactic Astronomy: Structure and Kinematics*, 2nd ed. (1981), is a thorough, mathematically replete textbook on the Milky Way Galaxy and other galaxies, with emphasis on structure and dynamics.

THE STUDY OF GALAXIES, GALAXIES OF MANY TYPES, AND GALAXIES OTHER THAN OUR OWN

William H. Waller and Paul W. Hodge, *Galaxies and the Cosmic Frontier* (2003), gives a thorough review of both the properties of galaxies and their relation to the wider questions of cosmology. Mark H. Jones and Robert J. Lambourne, *An Introduction to Galaxies and Cosmology* (2004), is a textbook intended for college students but that can be read to advantage by informed nonstudents. Linda S. Sparke and John S. Gallagher, *Galaxies in the Universe* (2000), is a very useful textbook designed for advanced undergraduate students and others with a knowledge of the basics of astronomy. Debra M. Elmegreen, *Galaxies and Galactic Structure* (1998), is a basic introduction with excellent nonmathematical treatment of almost all aspects of galactic and extragalactic subjects. Sidney van den Bergh, *Galaxy Morphology and Classification* (1998), is a comprehensive treatment of the subject, and *The Galaxies of the Local Group* (2000), is a complete treatment of the properties of the nearest galaxies. Edwin Hubble, *The Realm of the Nebulae* (1936, reprinted 1982), is a classic account of the early history of extragalactic research written by one of the pioneer investigators. Allan Sandage, *The Hubble Atlas of Galaxies* (1961), discusses galaxy classification and includes marvelous full-page illustrations of different types of galaxies.

INDEX

P

Q

S

T

U

V